PRAISE FOR
COMBAT TO CONSERVATION

"Here is a timeless tale, from Homer to Hemingway, of healing from war wounds by immersion in wilderness and wild nature. As a combat Marine in Vietnam in the early '70s, F. J. Fitzgerald was severely wounded and denied his dream of becoming a wildlife warden. He found solace in Northern Minnesota and in the wildness at the foot of the Sangre de Cristo range of Colorado. The wolves and lions he encountered there had the power to help heal his war wounds from the darker forests of his soul. His story is of a powerful mending."

—**Doug Peacock**, Author, Vietnam Veteran, Filmmaker, Naturalist

"This is a wonderful book. I personally have worked with Fitz, and the book reflects the high quality and grounded person I got to know and admire. I feel I had a parallel idyllic childhood as Fitz; both grew up on a MN farm, and we both ended up in the north woods. But unlike him, I didn't spend a harrowing time in Vietnam. I've spent a lifetime trying to portray the healing qualities of nature in my photographs and movies. Fitz's fine book perfectly illustrates that idea—nature can heal. I highly recommend it."

—**Jim Brandenburg**, Filmmaker and Best-Selling Author

"Hank Junior might have made popular the mantra 'A country boy can survive,' but Fitz has shown in a memoir that echoes the spirits of transcendentalists like Emerson and Thoreau that he can not only survive but thrive in the solace of our natural environment. With short, deliberately crafted brushstrokes, Fitz paints an inspirational canvas. After reading this journey from painful combat to newfound personal peace, you'll want to shut down your computer, charge up your digital camera, lace up your hiking boots, and find your best available hiking trail."

—**Matthew A. Tallon**, Co-Author of *100 Days in Vietnam: A Memoir of Love, War, and Survival*

"In life's great game of connect the dots, Fitz takes you along: from his prosaic childhood on the family farm to pivotal early hunting experiences, to riveting accounts of trauma and tragedy in Vietnam, and then landing on a deep passion for public lands and all things wild. His book, written with humility, honesty and integrity, draws you in to his lifelong evolving relationship with the natural world and its critical significance to our shared destiny."

—**Paul Schurke**, Wintergreen Adventures, Author, Educator, Arctic Explorer

"I actually teared up reading this. As a Catholic growing up in Middle America, playing in the woods, hunting, fishing, and enjoying the nature of our beautiful country, Francis delivers these memories, along with the realities of the lethal cauldron of Vietnam. I was not able to put this book down."

—**Master Sergeant (Retired) Nathan Aguinaga**, US Army, Four-Book Author, including *Division: Life on Ardennes Street*

"*Combat to Conservation* is a moving story of the interdependent relationship between people and nature. Sharing his personal experience, Fitzgerald makes a compelling case that people need nature for the well-being of our souls, and nature needs people to protect its very existence."

—**Sarah Strommen**, Commissioner, Minnesota
Department of Natural Resources

"This is an amazing story of the personal healing power of nature, but it is also an important call to action. Fitz reminds us that 'we can be that which holds the planet together and protects it' . . . but only if we are willing to fight for it."

—**Kris Larson**, Executive Director, Minnesota Land Trust

"Sometimes the baggage of our lives, emotional stress, and unexpressed feelings hide in the closet of our minds. Then, one day, bits and pieces of the past create an uneasiness, an emptiness that keeps us stuck in a post-traumatic mindset. In *Combat to Conservation*, author Francis Fitzgerald unlocks haunting memories of a young eighteen-year-old Marine facing combat in Vietnam. Witnessing the loneliness of war, his feelings of anger and hopelessness, Francis describes his return to home and recovery as he embraces the wilderness. In the solitude of a wildlife retreat, Francis finds a healing connection between the hunter and the conservationist. This is a compelling story of our relationship with the earth, each other, and the need for conservation. Our survival depends on this correlation."

—**Marilyn Gansel**, PsyD, Positive Performance
Coach, Co-Author of *Saved by Sport*

Combat to Conservation: A Marine's Journey through Darkness into Nature's Light

by F. J. Fitzgerald

© Copyright 2022 F. J. Fitzgerald

ISBN 978-1-64663-637-2

Published by

köehlerbooks™

3705 Shore Drive
Virginia Beach, VA 23455
800-435-4811
www.koehlerbooks.com

To Leaky! Thanks for all the old times!

COMBAT *to* CONSERVATION

A Marine's Journey through Darkness
into Nature's Light

F. J. FITZGERALD

VIRGINIA BEACH
CAPE CHARLES

TABLE OF CONTENTS

To the 58,220 Soldiers, Marines, Sailors and Airmen who never had a chance to write a book about this.

ONE STORMY NIGHT

January 1951

L ots of snow and wind created massive drifts across the semi-open landscape. On January 13, 1951, when I decided to make my move into this crazy world, winter was brutal and in full swing. Somehow my father managed to get Mom from the farm to Rochester to St. Mary's Hospital. In those days, a mother and baby were hospitalized for a few days, nothing like today's fast turnaround. By the time Mom and I were ready to go home, the big black 1947 Pontiac couldn't cut the drifts, and according to my best sources, Dad could only get us halfway home and had to meet Mom and I with a horse and sleigh. Thus, the title for my sixth grade autobiography naturally became "One Stormy Night." My siblings tell me I was spoiled early on because, after my two older brothers, there had been a run of three girls in the family, and I was the welcome addition that evened the ratio out once again. The boys became the bookends of the family.

My earliest memories from the big farm are looking out the upstairs window of the farmhouse watching my two older brothers heading down to the barn in the morning. Why that scene sticks in my head, who knows, but I see it over and over again when I think about the big farm. Maybe I was jealous and wanted to go with them, I don't know, or maybe I heard them getting up and wanted to see what was going on. I'm not sure how old I was at the time. I remember watching the coal truck come to the house and dump coal for the furnace down the chute into the crude basement, and how warm it was there when the fire was stoked. We had a chamber pot in the pantry of the kitchen so the kids didn't have to use the outhouse in bad weather. I slept upstairs, most likely in my brother's room, after I graduated from a crib.

Later on, I remember watching Dad chasing a snapping turtle with a pitchfork out of the barnyard and away from the chickens, back toward the creek, and the two dogs staying just out of reach of the turtle's lunges. We had a big white barn, and I liked to go up in the haymow and play, but only when Dad and my brothers were downstairs milking because I was a little scared of that dark and spooky place. We always had cats around the barn, and my brothers use to scare me and tell me there was a huge stray tomcat up there that was as big as the dogs. So, I spent a lot of time sitting on the top rung of the ladder, looking into the haymow, ready for a quick exit.

I remember Dad warning me about never going into the bullpen behind the barn, as we had a large ornery Holstein bull there that even my brothers were afraid of. So, I would sneak over and stand on the safe side of the fence and taunt the bull and send in Lad, our collie, to harass it.

Most of the time, I was within earshot of the house, out exploring in the huge yard and woods around the buildings. Sticks were my earliest weapons in those days, and many a stick was used to poke into the weeds and brush all around the farm. I always had the big collie at my side, as we were inseparable. I remember the farm seemed so big, as it was my entire world at the time. I still have a soft spot for collies. A highlight a couple times a week was running up the hill behind the house and across the field to watch the train pass by. We had a half-wild Shetland pony that we all tried to ride with little success, especially when he knew the train was coming!

One of the best memories was Christmas Eve Mass at St. Bridget's Catholic Church a few miles from the farm, in a setting right out of a Currier and Ives painting. That old country church is still there and is one of the few constants that remain the same after all these years. I believe all seven of us were baptized there, and my parents and oldest brother are buried there in the beautiful country setting.

I never found out why Mom and Dad decided to move off the farm and into town. I imagine the fact that the new airport was being built close by and a superhighway called Interstate 90 cut the acreage in half and made it impractical to farm were reasons enough. Both of my brothers were getting ready to leave for college, and I'm guessing that also played a role in making the decision. I just remember that I didn't want to move.

I was five going on six when we moved into NW Rochester. We bought a new house, just finished, on the last street in town. A new high school was under construction at the time, and the site was a good distraction for me. I had never seen so much sand and rock and large equipment, which was literally across the street. Days were spent riding my bike around the construction site and the edge of town. There were corn fields and woods just to the north where I could go and watch the deer, geese, fox, and pheasants, and mess around with my newfound friends of the neighborhood.

Our block was full of young families with lots of kids, so making friends was easy. Endless games of pickup baseball in the street and chasing around after dark got to be routine. There was a new Catholic grade school three short blocks from the house that my sisters and I attended, and a public school a block from that. So, the entire neighborhood gang either walked or rode our bikes to school every day during the warmer weather. In winter, we would bundle up like Eskimos and walk, getting all sweaty by the time we arrived at school.

We never locked up our bikes, as there was no need to. Occasionally, someone would move a bike from one end of the bike rack to the other so the kid would have to look for it among dozens and dozens of bikes at school. Stealing a bike was unheard of back then. I remember each time I moved up a size in bikes, going from a fifteen-inch to a twenty-inch to a big twenty-four-inch bike. I remember the twenty-four incher the best because that was my first brand new bike, a shiny black Western Auto with red trim and a rack on the back. But I kept my twenty-incher for beating around the woods.

We never got an allowance, like most of our friends did, and there weren't a lot of chores to do in town, so our own money was hard to come by. Birthdays and holidays were about it, with an occasional first communion or confirmation adding to the pot. Somehow, I talked Mom into giving me some of the S&H Green Stamps she would get at the Piggly Wiggly. It took forever, but my first starter HO train set was from the stamp store. I still have it to this day. Life was simple and good.

BACK TO THE COUNTRY

My family only stayed in town for a few years of my life. Sometimes your soul knows where it belongs early in life—and I already knew. We moved back out into the country when I was around nine or ten. The small city of forty thousand was okay, but as the city flourished and grew, I would have to ride my bike farther and farther to find the woods and fields that I craved. When Mom and Dad bought a farm around five miles out of town, I was overjoyed with the return of outdoor opportunities and adventures. Our farm was mostly pasture and hayfields with an occasional corn or soybean year. But it backed up to hundreds of acres of hardwood forests ripe for my daily adventures.

Aside from the daily chores I had, which I loved, I lived and breathed to be outside in the fields, fence lines, woods, and windbreaks. There was so much to see. I didn't miss the neighborhood at all. Suddenly, after those few years in town, it seemed like wildlife was everywhere.

Early mornings and evenings were my favorite time of day. I would spend hours sneaking along the edges, sitting to watch deer, fox, pheasants, birds, striped gophers, and even an occasional coyote, and I would find myself imagining I was watching and studying timber wolves in the wild up north. Sometimes I would walk along with the cattle and blend in enough so the deer wouldn't run away. I was obsessed with wildlife and reading as much as possible about each species.

I trapped pocket gophers on the neighboring farms. The township still had a bounty on them, and it was easy money—not a lot of money, mind you, but easy. If I found a fresh mound from the night before, all I had to do was poke the hole with a stick and my dog would dig at it until it opened, and I could set the trap down in it. It was quite the system. If I recall, the bounty was fifteen cents a gopher, and all you had to do was prove your catch. That was accomplished by bringing in the front paws of the gopher. Every so often, a pair of gopher paws would accidentally go through the washing machine if Mom didn't check my jean pockets. She learned fast.

There was a small grove of trees about halfway back to the big woods on the farm along our fence line. When I could talk Mom into it, I would set up an old pup tent I bought at Sears and pretend I was way out West in the mountains, hunting and camping alone in the wild. It was the idea of being in the wild that I was so attracted to. Back in those years, the farm was my wild. My dog was usually with me, and we were living an adventure every day. Little did I realize that those early days of playing and exploring the countryside would lay the foundation for a lifelong passion for nature and the wilderness.

LITTLE GREEN MEN

Summer 1962

They were almost set in. Everyone's position technically perfect. Dug in for the night. Ready to strike down anything coming with their reach. Motionless in the darkness, waiting for the unknown. Then, without warning, the earth shakes. There's a thunderous noise as rocks fly. Nothing but dust and chaos.

I scream, "BAD DOG! I told you to keep the cows away from here." The collie runs in wagging her tail and stands next to me on a lush green hillside in a quiet pasture in southeast Minnesota.

As quickly as it starts, it's over. Dozens of little green men, plastic soldiers, purchased at Woolworths for ninety-nine cents a bag, lay strewed among the rocks and lush green vegetation. I pick up the pieces, some too broken to save, and dump them back in the bag, to go back home. Then, I'd pick up everything, move to a different spot, and start all over again.

THE HUNT

October 1966

M y freshman year in high school, I purchased a bow. It was a beautiful Indian recurve bow with gorgeous, laminated wood detail. I wanted to deer hunt and bring venison to the family. There was always meat in the freezer. I remember rationalizing with my mom. We raised beef cattle and shipped them to market; there was no difference between that and hunting on the farm. "And the deer are in your gardens constantly!"

I practiced in the barn and yard all summer and I became what I thought was a pretty good shot with a bow. When September came around, I purchased an archery deer license.

I knew the surrounding woods like the back of my hand. I knew every trail, every water seep, where they entered and exited the fields, and where they typically bedded. I practically lived in these woods. After school, I would sit out in the fence line or woodlot and wait, rehearsing the different scenarios in my mind.

After a few weeks, I was out one evening sitting in a small windbreak along the fence line. A major trail came through the woodlot and entered the cornfield. I brushed in a makeshift blind and waited. I knew from either direction I would have a clear shot.

It was starting to sprinkle, and I could hear distant thunder. My back sat against an old knotty fence post.

Shortly before dark, while I could still count the corn rows, a buck suddenly jumped the fence from behind and, out of nowhere, I was looking at my potential target, ten yards away. He had stopped to look into the cornfield before stepping out of the tree line. It was like he sensed something was not right. Instinctively, I drew back and released the cedar arrow. I heard it hit behind his shoulder and saw the blood squirt out. He ran down the edge of the field, stumbled, and fell twenty-five yards away. I waited just to make sure he didn't get up, then I slowly and quietly stepped out toward the body lying in the gentle rain. He quivered one last time, and I jumped back and raised the bow again. Then I realized I hadn't knocked another arrow, rookie mistake, but he was done.

I'll never forget the strange mix of feelings I suddenly had. Somehow this was different than the sparrows and gophers I had shot in the past. I had just shot and killed something much larger, something that, minutes before, was walking in his home environment without care or fear of who might lie in wait. I knelt beside him and pulled my arrow out of his side. I still remember the smell of his warm blood that had soaked through the knees of my jeans, and the buck's strong musky scent. I brushed the dirt off his head and just sat there looking at him and touching his polished antler tips. It took forever to field dress the buck, as I had never done it before.

Then, like that, reality struck. I was a wild teenage kid who had just killed his first buck in my first year. I was now shaking from excitement and pride. I walked back home in the dark, with my bow over my shoulder, to get the tractor to bring him back home. I dragged him back to the barn and hung him up on a rafter, like I had seen in magazines. Dad came down to check him out. I was ecstatic, but I had no one to share the feeling with. No one in my family really celebrated with me, as they weren't hunters.

POPS

Dad was born in 1905. If he were alive at this writing, he would be 116 years old. I often think about the changes he saw over his lifetime. He literally lived from the horse-and-buggy days to the space-age. He lived through two world wars, the Great Depression, the Korean war, the Iron Curtain, and the Cold War, and then the Vietnam era. It was like he lived through his own version of the Industrial Revolution. He didn't marry until he was nearly thirty and met Mom, who was a teacher in a one room country school.

Soon after they got married, they took over the farm I was born on. Dad worked a lot. Besides farming, he always had another job. He was also older than most of my classmates' dads. Sometimes they would mistake him for my grandpa, but that never really bothered me. He was a genius at fixing things. It didn't matter if it was cars, trucks, tractors, or farm machinery. Anything mechanical, he would somehow figure out how to repair it. So, I was naturally drawn to tinkering with things too. It was something that, as I grew older, blended perfect with my independence and my wild streak. I loved to mow and bale hay, till the garden, feed the cattle and horses, and mow the thistles in the pasture, as it was a great opportunity to observe the wildlife. I felt good when Pops would come home at night and there was nothing left that had to be done. He could then eat supper, putz a bit outside in the barn or garage, then fall asleep in his chair watching Perry Como on TV or *Bonanza*.

He never really had hobbies. I guess his hobbies were the farm, the garden, and his family. He was witty, but quiet, clever, extremely patient, and a devout Catholic. Not bad qualities when you are raising seven children. Mom was always the disciplinarian, but we all knew Pops had her back. I don't ever remember being mad or upset at Dad. I would get mad at Mom for being too strict, but that's the cost of being the disciplinarian in the family. I just know I wanted to please Dad and make him happy and proud. I always wonder where I got my passion to hunt and fish, because he never hunted or fished. He did have an old Remington single shot .22 for sparrows and woodchucks. I still have it. Once in a while, he would talk about growing up in southeastern Minnesota in the bluffs and river valleys. He would speak about how he and his older brother would take turns sitting out at night to watch over the sheep and cattle if there were wolves or coyotes in the area. His parents died when he was young, so he lived with an aunt during high school. He never really talked much about his childhood. I wish I would have pressed him more to share it with me.

Both Mom and Dad loved trees, especially pines. So, we planted a lot of them. After a new tree was planted, it was nurtured, watered, fenced in from the deer, and guarded just until it could get along on its own. If they would find a young seedling, it was my job to dig away the weeds, water and fertilize it, and protect it like a Prodigal Son. I still catch myself doing that when I find a young white pine.

None of my family was ever in the military. I think about how shocked Mom and Dad must have been when I enlisted in the Marine Corps. They knew that 1969 was a bad time.

Dad had a couple bad heart attacks while I was in high school. He missed my high school graduation while recovering from one. He bounced back and lived for another thirty years. Mom was a stay-at-home mom. She never had a driver's license and was totally dependent on Dad for the sixty years of marriage. They were inseparable. They often held hands when walking around. If ever there was a role model couple, they were it.

I would think about them a lot when I was over in country. If I ever got married, I just really wanted my marriage to be like theirs—to love somebody that much.

Dad passed away on my oldest son's twenty-fourth birthday. He lived ninety-one years. I didn't cry at all during the entire funeral. I kept it together for a few days afterwards, then, one afternoon, I walked out into the woods, sat under a large white pine, and wept. I don't ever cry much. I still don't, But that day, I wept.

A few days later, I planted a new white pine.

SIGNING UP

Summer of 1969

"Only those who risk going too far can possibly find out how far they can go."

—TS Elliot

Following high school, I was working the graveyard shift at a shitty dairy job. I wanted to go to college to be a game warden, but I knew I wasn't ready and would probably screw up something. I really couldn't afford to screw up. One afternoon, I was downtown and saw recruiting posters by the post office. Even though I had a partial academic-athletic scholarship for college, something pulled me inside. I remember walking up the big marble steps and going down a hallway toward the recruiting offices. I walked right past the Army, Navy, and Air Force offices, and into the Marine Corps recruiter's office. A sergeant and a staff sergeant were casually sitting in there talking while I sort of browsed around looking at the information and posters. I honestly don't recall any pressure from either of them. To the contrary, they were relaxed. We talked a bit about the options of enlistment and delayed-enlistment terms, and I left without even a brochure. For the next couple days, I researched and read everything I could get my hands on about the Marine Corps. I went to the library and then read everything about it in our encyclopedia Britannica at home in my bedroom. I read about Bella Woods in WWI, Iwo Jima in WWII, the Chosen Reservoir in

Korea, and countless other theatres in which the Marines would overcome against terrible odds. *The Few, the Proud.* All of this, of course, triggered the interest and curiosity of an eighteen-year-old kid not quite ready for college. It only made sense that if you are going to join the military, then clearly it had to be the Marine Corps. The Marines were the best.

By the end of the week, I had pretty much convinced myself to sign up, even with the reality of the Vietnam War on TV every night. It was a challenge of a lifetime, a challenge I couldn't resist. And it would certainly improve the possibility of becoming a game warden after college. A few days later, I walked up the same marble stairway and into the same office with the same two Marines, and I signed up for the delayed-entry program for a three-year enlistment. Delayed entry, so I could have a few weeks to do whatever I wanted to do before I left for boot camp.

I never told them directly, because I knew Mom and Dad would be heartbroken and shocked and frightened. So, I wrote a letter and had my little sister give it to them while they were on a short vacation with the oldest brother. Kind of a shitty thing to do, but I thought it would be better if they had some time before I spoke to them.

I took a road trip out West, and a few weeks later, I jumped on a Greyhound bus at the old train station in Rochester for Minneapolis and was sworn into the United States Marine Corps the next day. That evening, I boarded my first jet airplane and flew to San Diego, California, to the Marine Corps Recruit Training Depot, and there began a new chapter in my life.

THE MOUNTAINS

September 1969

*"The world is a book, and those who do not travel read
only one page."*

—St. Augustine

The few weeks I had before reporting, I drove out to see the
Rocky Mountains. A buddy of mine was going to come along,
but he backed out. So, I went anyway, alone. Dad and I gave
my car a good inspection and two new tires before I headed west on
Interstate 90, destination the largest mountain range in the country.

I had never driven alone more than a couple hours to the Twin
Cities. I was super excited to be driving alone on a cross country trip
to the mountains. I would camp along the way in the same crappy
little pup tent I had at the farm. After studying the state farm road
atlas my dad let me borrow, I decided my destination was going to
be Colorado and Rocky Mountain National Park.

The plains took forever to drive across, but then on a sunny
bright afternoon, I looked ahead at what I first thought were clouds,
but it was in fact the mountains on the horizon. Little did I realize
they were still a day's drive away.

I didn't sleep much that night. In fact, I didn't even set up my
tent. All I could think about was driving into the mountains that
next day. At first light, I was heading toward the foothills. I realized
I had left my transistor radio on the picnic table at the campsite,

but I couldn't get myself to turn around and go back and get it. At a gas station in Colorado, I saw a USMC bumper sticker and bought it. But afterwards, I remembered what the recruiter had said about earning the title of *Marine*, so I never put it on the car, but the pride was already setting in.

The last evening before the mountains, I camped at a reservoir somewhere in east-central Colorado. It was a large lake with rip rap boulders around the shoreline. I found a flat spot in the rubble and set up my tent. Shortly afterward, an old local came down to fish from the shoreline. We talked for a bit, and then he asked me if I was planning on sleeping there. I told him yes and that I planned on heading into the mountains early in the morning. I remember him looking at me and saying, "Well, son, at night after dark, the rattlesnakes come down out of the hills and drink at the lake." He said he wouldn't be anywhere near the water at dusk. That's all it took, and I was packing up the old Plymouth and slept in the car that night. At dawn, after a nearly sleepless night in the car, I set out for the mountains.

Rocky Mountain National Park was another world to me—a flatlander kid suddenly in one of the most beautiful places in the country. I had never been to a national park. I slowly drove into the park, gaining elevation with every minute, and settled at the first campground I found—Timber Creek Campground. That's where I would see my first bull elk.

I had set up the tent along the creek at the back of the campground. Across the creek was a large open meadow guarded by a tall dark line of fir and pine. I had a pair of cheap binoculars, a Kodak Instamatic camera, and a can of 7 UP. I would wait for days if I had to; I just wanted to see something new—a mountain animal. I watched two coyotes mousing in the tall grass, fished for trout, and sat on a rock for hours each day, looking across the creek and down at water. I didn't mind waiting because I was in heaven. The first large animals I saw were a couple mule deer does, and I quickly spotted the difference in the size of the ears compared to our Minnesota white tails. I continued my vigilance and fished the hours away.

I don't recall how many days it took, but one evening, right around dusk, I was scanning the tree line when something filled my field of vision. A large bull elk walked out of the dark timber and stood in the meadow. He was huge, and the most magnificent animal I had ever seen. I can still close my eyes and see him today. The creek, the meadow, the dark timber line, and that beautiful, majestic bull elk. I was awestruck at the size of his antlers, dark milk chocolate brown with white dagger-like tips at the ends. It was then, at that very moment, that I was forever hooked on the beauty of this heavenly place I only learned of a few days before. I knew then I wanted to study natural resources the rest of my life, a feeling inside me all along. How else could I explain my love of the outside, the animals, the silence, and wild places? All it took was one elk, one stream, and the Rocky Mountains.

Countless times when I was over in country, I would think about that quiet stream, the sounds, the smells, and those trout, as I filled my canteen with water or dunked my head in a cool mountain stream in the Que Son Mountains in South Vietnam. A world so far away from those Rockies. But this was a dark, dangerous, and different world now.

I promised myself I would get back and see that beautiful world again.

THE IRISH
CATHOLIC FAMILY

There were seven children in our family, three boys and four girls. I was second to the youngest, and the youngest boy. With a span of over fifteen years between the oldest and the youngest children, I hardly remember the four oldest siblings being at home. As strange as it seems, I never really knew my older siblings until my adult life.

It was my oldest brother, Tom, who I got to know first when I was a young adult. He happened to be the oldest in the family, and much to my parents' wishes, he went to the seminary and became a Catholic priest. So, because he didn't have a family of his own, I spent more time with him when he was available. Priests were moved around frequently in those days, and he would be assigned new parishes across the southern part of Minnesota. For a few different assignments, he was in our hometown. That made it easy to spend time with him at Mom and Dad's on his days off from his priestly duties.

Tom wasn't exactly a normal priest, at least from my perspective. He owned a snowmobile, a dirt bike, loved fishing, and drove a 4X4 Chevy Blazer among other rigs, and he was a pilot. We spent a lot of time together during my high school years.

One hot summer day, when I was mowing the lawn on the farm, he brought me out a beer. That was huge, because there was never alcohol in the house. Only *Father Tom*, as we called him, could get by with such a bold move.

It was only fitting then that I deliberately stopped by to visit him on my way back from my mountain trip after graduation and before bootcamp. I limped into Worthington, Minnesota, where he was assigned at the time, with a leaky water pump on my old Plymouth Valiant. After a quick trip to Champion Auto, we replaced it in the church parking lot the next morning. I spent another night there, and he took me up in a Cessna 150 for a flight over the area. That was the first time I had ever been in an airplane. A month later I would board a jet for San Diego. My first commercial flight was to the Marine Corps Recruit Depot and USMC bootcamp.

I would miss the talks that Tom and I had about everything from God to sports cars, and when I was in country, out on a listening post, sitting and waiting for an ambush, or in a hole somewhere on perimeter security, I would think about those discussions. His opinions were always straightforward and honest, and he sometimes surprised me when he held nothing back. There was no difference in his response, whether he was speaking as a brother or a priest. That was the beauty of it.

When I was wounded, it was Father Tom that took charge and contacted the Red Cross and somehow tracked me down at the military hospital in Yokosuka, Japan. I was still heavily sedated, and I don't remember much about that call, but I do remember him coming right out and asking "Well, are you all there?" That was his not-so-subtle way of asking if I had all my body parts. He was a tremendous help and support for my parents at that grave time. I'm not sure how they would have dealt with my situation without him. After I was flown to Great Lakes Naval Hospital, near Chicago, he drove Mom and Dad down for their first visit. After a few months, when I could leave for the weekend, he would drive down, pick me up, and then take me back and forth to home.

Over the next few years, we continued to stay close and were each other's sounding board for anything that was bothering us. No topic was off limits, from celibacy to premarital sex. I know it meant a lot to him that I treated him like a friend *and brother* rather than a priest up on a pedestal.

Then one day:

> *"The Rev. Thomas P. Fitzgerald, forty-one, pastor of Sacred Heart Church in Brewster, Minnesota, a Rochester native and former pastor at St. Pius X Catholic here, died unexpectedly Thursday afternoon with an apparent heart attack.*
>
> *He was born Jan. 10, 1938, in Rochester, attended Immaculate Heart of Mary Seminary in Winona and graduated from St. Mary's College in Winona in 1960. He studied theology at Mount St. Bernard Seminary in Dubuque, Iowa, and was ordained a priest for the Diocese of Winona on May 24, 1964. He then served in parishes in La Crescent, Hokah, Worthington, St. Pius X in Rochester, and in Winona until his assignment to Brewster in July of 1978."*

It was a shock to us all when he passed away suddenly. My parents never really got over it. Even after Vietnam, it was the hardest loss I ever went through.

To this day, I still talk to him often.

TRAIN LONG, TRAIN HARD

Fall 1969

I was in really good shape, I thought. I had run track and cross country during high school, did the farm chores and lifted weights at home. But nothing can prepare you for Marine Corps boot camp. The physical, mental, and emotional shock was intense. But before long, as I watched some recruits break down under the psychological pressures of the drill instructors, I soon came to grips with myself and realized it was as much a mental training as a physical one. After that, it was a breeze, albeit with a few hiccups. I weighed around 153 pounds going into boot camp and graduated at a lean and mean 175.

During the day, you didn't have time to think about anything. But night was different, and the ugly fear of the unknown would creep into your mind every now and then while in your rack.

Shortly before graduation one night, the DI had us all sit on the floor of the barracks as he read off each Marines MOS (Military Occupational Specialty).

Private Fitzgerald . . . 0311 . . . Infantry . . . you're a GRUNT.

Now, as a new Marine Corps grunt, with Nam raging wild, there was a pretty good chance of seeing it up close and personal, as we used to say. But by then my mental toughness was at a peak, so the plan seemed simple: I'd go over, rack up some nice combat pay, send it home, buy a nice car when I got back, and start college. Thank God that's how an eighteen-year-old thinks.

A couple of occasions during boot camp, I was called in and approached about other potential *opportunities* available in the Corps. After going through your records, if certain things stood out, you would be interviewed about these additional opportunities. You never knew what the meeting would yield, but it was a great chance to skip training that day, get a decent meal, and hear what they had to say. The first *opportunity* presented itself one night after chow. We were in the barracks and the DIs were messing with us when the head DI came out of his office and called me forward. "Private Fitzgerald, tomorrow morning at 0800 you are going to go and try out for the Marine Corps band. Now isn't that nice. So, ladies, while Private Fitzgerald is over there in a cushy little place tooting his little horn, trying out for the band, you all are going to do extra PT because he will miss his PT in the morning!"

The glares were unbearable, but I knew each one of those guys would kill for the chance to get out of hell for a morning. I slept with one eye open that night.

I guess they had noticed from my records that I had played the saxophone during school and would be interested in auditioning for a chance to change MOS and join the Marine Corps band. So, the next morning, I found myself in line, with a government saxophone, for an audition. I hadn't picked up a saxophone in six months, but I guess it's sort of like riding a bicycle. I did great, as the audition was easy. But just a couple days later, I turned down the opportunity to join the band and see the world. It just wasn't the direction I needed to go. Upon returning to the barracks, I immediately had to do pushups until the DI got tired of watching me and said stop. When I told him I turned it down, he made me do more pushups, and called me a dumb SOB. My only regret to this day is that my favorite teacher, my high school band director, would have been so proud had one of his students made the Marine Corps band.

The next opportunity presented itself when our platoon was gathered together in a classroom listening to a presentation on first aid in the battlefield. After the class ended, a few of us were told to remain in the room, and a major came in and briefed us about Officer Candidate School.

Now this intrigued me as I listened to a major talk about how we were selected. Our high school or college records showed a high GPA, which meant great leadership potential. The deal breaker for me was that I would have to sign up for an additional four years.

No thanks, looks like Vietnam it is!

After twelve weeks of boot camp, we were ready to receive our Eagle, Globe, and Anchor. Graduation from Marine Corps boot camp is a big deal, even to the DIs. They get to march down the parade field and show off their platoons of new Marines in front of the brass and invited friends and relatives of the recruits. There is a reception afterwards, and for the first time, we were given an on base liberty for the rest of the day. My parents didn't come. I know they never realized the importance of the day, and they probably hated the idea because they imagined what was to come. It was a bittersweet day for me, as a couple of us were alone, without family, and headed back to the barracks. It was one of the loneliest days of my life. But I had never felt prouder inside.

A grunt automatically moved on to months of additional training, and toward the end of advanced infantry training, a couple of us applied for recon school. Three of us got accepted. I knew where I was headed, so the more training I could get, the better. I also hoped it would mean shipping out with other Recon Marines. Graduation from recon school was another proud day for me.

After that, we were granted our first leave to go home. It was spring and I had missed Christmas, so we had it all over again. The leave was a little less than thirty days, and it went by extremely fast.

I don't honestly remember what I did during those short days. I do remember going out to the local junior college and catching up with some high school buddies. I also spent some time with my girlfriend and my siblings. I walked around in the woods around the farm and just enjoyed the peace and quiet. I spent a lot of time trying to convince my parents that it would be okay, and I would be back soon to start college. They didn't buy that idea at all. I went to church in uniform and felt very proud to be wearing the Eagle, Globe, and Anchor. In a few short weeks, I flew back to Camp Pendleton to whatever waited.

Then it was off to staging in Okinawa. Staging was weird. After a long flight from California, you pretty much just got gear, did PT, and waited around until your orders came through. Waiting was hard. As good Marines, we were ready to go *in country*.

ESCALATION

March 1965

I t was five years earlier when the war erupted in full blossom. Military Java Group accounts boiled it down succinctly:

The USS Henrico, Union, and Vancouver, carrying the 9th Marine Expeditionary Brigade take up stations four thousand yards off Red Beach Two, just north of Da Nang, South Vietnam. Two old WWII vintage attack transport ships and a new era amphibious transport dock ship were now there making history.

First ashore was the Battalion Landing Team 3/9, which arrived on the beach at 8:15 AM. Wearing full battle gear and carrying M14s, the Marines were met by sightseers, South Vietnamese Officers, Vietnamese girls with leis, and four American soldiers with a large sign saying "Welcome, Gallant Marines." General William Westmoreland, senior US military commander in Saigon, was reportedly "appalled"' at the spectacle because he had hoped the Marines could land without any fanfare. Within two hours, Battalion Landing Team 1/3 began landing at the Da Nang airbase. The thirty-

five hundred Marines were deployed to secure the US airbase, supposedly freeing up the South Vietnamese troops for combat.

It was later that same month, further south and west, the 325th Division of the North Vietnamese Regular Army (the NVA), consisting of three regiments, totaling about five thousand men, quietly infiltrated from Laos into South Vietnam. They would eventually meet as the die was cast. Military Java posted this account:

It took the members of the 9th Marine Expeditionary Brigade almost an entire day to bring their men and materials ashore that day in March 1965. Nguyen Tien knows, because he was there.

Nguyen was twenty-four at the time but had already been a Viet Cong gorilla for five years, and he was on the beach that morning to spy on the Americans. He says they were carrying too much gear and were sweating like pigs. How, he thought to himself, are they going to be able to fight in this heat?

But he also knew American Marines meant trouble. He knew these weren't French soldiers.

"When I saw the Americans arrive, I knew war was about to get harder; it was going to be more ferocious, and it was going to last a lot longer," he says. "A lot more people were going to die, and if we weren't very determined, we weren't going to win."

WELCOME TO THE NAM

May 1970

"Innocence is not knowing what to fear."

—FF

After years of sending supplies, conducting airstrikes, and having advisors in Vietnam, the first combat troops to land on the beach were, of course, Marines, approximately thirty-five hundred who landed, amphibious style, on a beach, in Da Nang.

Five years later, I remember looking out the window of the commercial jet. I could see the coast and the waves breaking and washing onto the beach, just like any other ocean-side city. But this was the coastline of the Republic of South Vietnam.

The word was that Da Nang was pretty secure—at the air base, at least. We had flown a charter jet from Okinawa to Da Nang, with a regular civilian crew. I could see the uncomfortable looks on the faces of the stewardess as we silently walked past them to disembark from the jet. When I think of it now, what could they have said? What could you possibly say to a bunch of eighteen- and nineteen-year-old Marines heading into one of the cruelest wars in history? It was better that they simply remained silent.

As I approached the door, I remember it feeling like someone opened a blast furnace and told us to step inside. The temperature was overwhelming. By the time we reached the bottom of the stairs and stepped on the ground of the airstrip, we were already sweating profusely. The smell was a combination of jet exhaust, diesel fuel, hot concrete, and an indescribable mix of sweat and smoke.

Huge steel and concrete buildings lined the runways as we stood in line to get mustered in. Sandbag bunkers were everywhere. I had no idea what time it was, but we were all hungry, and wanted gear before chow.

So, I stood there, sweating my ass off, wondering, *Does this place get attacked? Should we really be just standing in line here without a weapon? What if there is an attack or a mortar barrage?* I looked around and saw three large sandbag bunkers, a couple watch towers, and then heard a gunship fly over. Without realizing it, my survival instincts had already kicked in.

As our names were called off, we busted ranks and followed. We walked into a large warehouse filled with lines of tables and shelves. As we were issued our gear, my heart relaxed a bit. Last up, we signed out our M16 with six empty magazines. I honestly don't remember if we eventually received rounds for our magazines that day. I don't even recall eating that day. I just remember walking into a large barracks and popping up on a top bunk exhausted, hanging my gear off the bedpost. I left my jungles and boots on and eventually fell asleep.

Loud explosions woke me—not that I slept that much. Incoming mortar rounds. No one had talked about the *what-ifs* that night. My chest felt like it was going to explode, and I was not sure whether to stay or exit the building. Everyone had the same stunned look on their faces. About that time, a staff sergeant nonchalantly walked into the barracks and yelled, "It's okay girls, relax. It's just Charlie welcoming you to Vietnam."

Apparently, it was pretty much a nightly occurrence. Just a constant harassment of the airbase to let you know Charlie is always somewhere outside the wire. I didn't close my eyes the rest of that night.

I had never thought about it much until now, but I had never ridden in a helicopter until VN. Despite all that training we did, even recon school, we never trained with or from choppers. We would repel off towers, getting ready for the day that we might zip down from the choppers in a hot LZ, but not from the birds themselves.

My first ride was from staging at 1st Mar Div. in Da Nang, to the forward LZ and Fire Base where I was assigned—Fire Base Baldy. The chopper was a large CH-53 Sea Stallion, better known as the Jolly Green Giant, the first of many trips in the belly of those dark green monsters. We flew approximately thirty-three kilometers SSE of Da Nang. I was one of the last Marines to get on board, and I remember I could see out the back of the chopper over the hatch. I recall just a patchwork of greens and browns, water and rice paddies, and small villages. I would later realize a lot of what I was seeing were bomb craters and burnt vegetation. I don't recall being scared that day. Maybe I just wanted to get out of that place where we had our first mortar experience. I didn't realize it, but soon the bush would feel much more secure to me than any of those occupied areas.

I don't know how fast or high we were flying to get out there, but suddenly the aircraft banked and dropped altitude extremely fast. I would learn that landing out in the remote LZs and fire bases was risky, at best. There was no circling the area or much of an approach. The pilots wanted to get in and out as fast as possible. Charlie loved to take pot shots at those big birds coming in. We landed in a cloud of yellow smoke and dust. I hadn't taken my pack off, so I was up and out in a few seconds. The rest of the Marines got off, and mail bags and a few supplies were unloaded, and the Jolly Green Giant was gone.

LZ Baldy was the field Regimental HQ for the 7th Marines, 1st Marine Division. Most Fire Bases in the bush were basically a high hilltop bulldozed flat on top for artillery batteries, and a landing zone for helicopters. This was a little bigger than that. A staff sergeant met us and called out names, assigning us grunts to a company and platoon. There were probably thirty-five of us that got off the bird that day. I kept waiting for my name to be called, and soon I was that last one standing there.

"PFC Fitzgerald? Follow me," the sergeant barked.

The LZ was off to one side of the hill, and we walked a hundred meters or so to an area of large bunkers, plywood buildings, and a couple towers. There were no signs on anything, but when we approached one of the large bunkers, I noticed a flagpole with the colors and the Marine Corps flag. I followed him down and into the bunker.

Lt. Col. Albers was a tall, slim, older Marine with a high and tight gray haircut. The staff sergeant pointed over to him and left. I wasn't quite sure what to do next. *Do I just wait here? Do I walk over and salute and report name, rank, and serial number? What the hell!*

Before I could make a move, the lieutenant colonel looked my way and waved me over.

He was standing in front of a huge map covering the wall at one end of the bunker. He reached out a hand, I saluted, and then I clumsily shook his hand.

For the next half hour or so, he explained that he or another officer perused the records of most Marines that are assigned to the command. They had noticed a few things in my file:

1. I had a good GPA in high school.
2. I had just completed recon school.
3. I had been offered Officers Candidate School and turned it down.

He wanted to know why I turned down Officers Candidate School. I told him I wasn't sure, but right now I wanted to try and get assigned to a Recon Battalion. I don't even recall his reaction to that, but I remember him saying that he wanted me in HQ S-2, S-3. I had no idea what that meant, but I figured that I should accept.

I was assigned to field HQ 2nd Battalion 7th Marines, S2, S3. So, for the next couple months, I lived on the LZ in a sort of bunker/tent with a plywood top, with a couple other HQ marines. In the command bunker, all the operations for missions and what we called *night acts* were platted on the map with corresponding grid coordinates. Those locations were then sent out via field radio to the units. These then became the locations for patrols, night ambushes, and various other missions for the day. Each night the location of every squad and platoon in the bush was plotted on the map. So, if something happened, their location was known for either ground support or fire-base support. Little did I know at the time how important that experience would prove to be. It was interesting once you got the hang of calculating the locations with the assigned grid numbers and carefully plotting those locations on the big map in the bunker. All daily incident reports were also called in and documented for the official record. Statistics like enemy contact, numbers of enemy, both enemy and friendly KIAs, and any other important information, such as caches, were all radioed in and recorded.

When not on duty in the bunker, we were responsible for perimeter watch at night along the edge of the hill, on various patrols sent out from the hill, or manning listening posts outside the perimeter at night. During any large battalion-size operations, the HQ would move out and set up closer to the operational area.

There was always the regular mortar harassment and periodic probing of the perimeter wire by the VC. Those weeks passed by, and that's when I started realizing that I felt more secure in the bush, outside the perimeter, rather than being a sitting duck in a large compound in the middle of nowhere, many kilometers from anything.

I started requesting more patrols, giving up my shifts in the bunker, volunteering for off the LZ listening posts, and eventually search-and-destroy patrols into the surrounding valleys.

About that time, I got the news that I would have to re-up for four more years to get reassigned to a Force Recon unit. I was disappointed but not ready to commit to four more years until I really had a feel for it. Then, one day, the lieutenant colonel called us in and informed us that the 7th Marines were pulling out of VN. We were fired up, but we weren't sure what that exactly meant. Did that mean we were all going back stateside? Within a couple days, reality struck, and anyone who wasn't a short timer would be reassigned. In other words, basically, the 7th Marine colors and command went home, and everyone else got transferred to other units. I never saw Lt. Col. Albers again. I was out on patrol the day he flew out. I found out later, he left me a great recommendation for the records. The rest of the guys got split up, depending on their MOS. Some of us were simply assigned to units of the 1st Marine Division, which took over responsibility of the 7th Marines. I got assigned to infantry with the 1st Marine Division, and chapter two of my tour began.

FIREFIGHT

Summer 1970

S weat stings your eyes as you walk on and on through endless tunnels of green. Everything is damp and dripping. *Eyes ahead, eyes down, eyes ahead, eyes down.* It had just stopped raining and the hot broiling sun steams you into a sweaty filthy stinking android, waiting for a break in the day, halfway to somewhere, in the middle of nowhere, but still a couple clicks away. You are not on point today, so it seems almost casual—if not for the heat and that raw itchy jock rash you've had for the last couple days. You would easily kill for a pair of new dry socks.

Something zips by and smacks a tree behind you. It sounds like a whip, only at three thousand feet per second. Then more and more. You realize in that instant its *contact*. You hit the ground and roll to the side of the trail as much as you dare. The staccato of small arms fire, and a rain of leaves and debris fills the air around you. Fucking Charlie had decided to make contact.

Everyone snaps into fight mode. Where's it coming from? Suppress the fire.

Is it coming from only one direction?

If someone has the *60* saturate the area ahead. Unconsciously, I press the mag release, drop the mag, and slap another one in. *How many do I have?*

Keep it on semi; don't fall for the temptation to pop it on auto. Who's got the blooper?

Who threw those frags; were they ours or theirs?

Where the hell is the radioman?

Who's got the rear?

Is it just a rag tag squad of VC, or did we make contact with a large group of NVA regular gooks?

Cease fire; save your ammo. So far, everything is hitting all around me. *Where's the fucking map so someone can call in support?*

Then as fast as it started, it's over. The air is saturated with the smell of gun powder. It's too quiet. *Don't get up yet. Did anyone actually see anything? Did anyone get hit? Are the sneaky little bastards gone? Is the point man down?* God, I hate the stinking quiet. *Another hit-and-run like usual? Or are they just waiting for us to relax and start moving around?*

The same thing, over and over, each time.

LITTLE GREEN MEN II

Summer of 1970

Finally, dusk, and the relentless burning sun slowly and reluctantly tucks below the ridge line. We are nearly set up. Foxholes dug, magazines out, grenades lined up in the dirt. As the sun sets, we slowly blend into the muted greens and browns and become a part of the environment we hate so much, hoping our dirty, sweat-stained camouflage matches the damp jungle ground. Anxious, heart pounding, ready, nervous, but not really scared, as we have done this countless times. It's almost like I sometimes feel safer under the dark cover of night.

Then, without warning, the earth shakes and heaves. Rocks, dirt, and debris flies everywhere. Hot metal. The noise is deafening as RPGs drop out of the sky. Death, out of nowhere. Someone screams, then, as sudden as it began, it's over. You wait and wait. *Are they just marking our position?* You wait for the assault. *Where the hell are they? Come on, you fuckers, give us a shot.* Nothing. *How the hell did they know we were here?*

Green men scattered around. Some lay strewed among the rocks and burnt vegetation. Some move, but most don't. Most are still afraid to move. Slowly we get up and crawl out of our holes and start picking up the pieces. The radioman grabs the handset to call in a Medi Vac bird. The enemy didn't stay around long enough to get chased away.

Some of ours would be too broken to save. We wrap them up in the bag to send them home. Then, we pick up the rest of our gear, move out to a new spot, and start all over again.

DIRTY ROTTEN SCOUNDREL

Fall 1970

We are promised fresh socks and a resupply if we hump back to Fire Base Ross by tomorrow.

Napoleon is thought to have once said, "An army marches on its stomach."

Marines march on their feet! As strange as it sounds, I never once rode in a ground vehicle anywhere in Vietnam. That could have been the nature of my tour, but I never sat in a Jeep, 6x6, tank, or any other form of truck. If we didn't take chopper, we walked. And walk we did.

You soon realize that your feet and your legs are the most vulnerable and the most important part of your body. From the jungles, to the mountains, to the jungle in the mountains, to the rice paddy dikes, or in the dirty rice paddy, the exposure to various environmental and climatic elements can quickly take a toll on your body, especially your feet. Constant exposure to water in the rice paddies, to streams in the mountains, and rivers in the valleys, and just the constant sweat, can tear up your feet and turn them into wet, wilted, soggy, painful, macerated, infected, ulcerated, sweaty stumps. Then rocks, mud, leeches, razor sharp vegetation, heat and rain, and insect bites add to the never-ending misery.

According to Wikipedia, a French army doctor first described the condition in 1812 and called it *trench foot*. It occurs when feet are continually exposed to damp, wet, unsanitary, and cold or hot conditions. Soggy boots in the jungle all day and night are a perfect petri dish for what was called *tropical ulcer*, or *jungle rot*, in Vietnam.

Here are the steps to treat jungle rot, trench foot, tropical ulcer, or whatever else you want to call it. Again, summarized from Wikipedia:

1. Thoroughly clean and dry your feet daily.
2. Put on clean, dry socks daily.
3. Treat the affected part by applying warm packs or soaking in warm water (102-110 degrees) for approximately five minutes.
4. When sleeping and resting, do not wear socks.
5. Obtain medical assistance as soon as possible.

That sounds great if I happen to contract a case while working at Microsoft in Silicon Valley, but humping the mountains and jungles of Vietnam, not so easy. I had yet to come across a spa.

So, when the tissue between your toes swells up and burns, eventually cracking open and peeling, oozing puss, you have a good classic case of *the rot*. Some guys seemed to be more susceptible to it than others. Some guys were medevacked time and again because of it. I had a real good friend from training and recon school who spent more time on the *SS Sanctuary* Hospital ship in China Beach than in the bush because of it. He couldn't help it.

In the bush, we'd remove boots and socks regularly, wring our socks out and dry them in the sun before putting them back on. That sounds easy, but rest stops and potty breaks aren't in the cards most of the time when you're humping three or five clicks on a search-and-destroy mission. You never want to get caught in a firefight barefoot. The standard-issue jungle boot would dry out amazingly quick if given a chance, but chances of that happening were few and far between. So, night became the time to take off the boots and socks and attempt to dry them out while sitting in a freshly dug out foxhole—until it rained.

I also had two very good reasons NOT to do that very often—snakes and Charlie.

I hated snakes. I still do. I feel guilty, because as a biologist, I should embrace them. But back then, I hated hearing stories about snakes during training, I hated thinking about snakes all the time, and I absolutely hated the thought of picking up my boots to find a little green viper had taken up residence. Without thinking, I would pick up the boot, hold it out away from my body, and turn it upside down to see what would fall out. Even then, there was no guarantee that whatever could be in there would just fall out, so I would take my kbar and probe my boot before looking inside, pounding like hell on the bottom of the boot. It usually worked.

The second reason that I hated taking my boots off at night was pretty obvious. Charlie liked to probe the lines in darkness in search of a weak point to slip in and raise hell. And as I already said, who wants to get in the shit with your boots off? And don't even think about taking off anything while sitting out somewhere on a night ambush.

Asking for a care package from home with foot powder could help, but it still had to reach you out in the middle of nowhere—and not get stolen.

So now you know why the idea of humping a few clicks to Fire Base Ross for the remote chance of getting new socks was a no brainer.

(We got there and I scored on some socks, not new, but washed and dry. I traded eight packs of smokes for a pair of clean USMC-issued, green, of course, socks.)

There are no winners in war.
For the soldier,
There is no end to a war.
It never retreats forever,
It never raises a white flag.
There is no armistice.
Only short periods of distractions push it to the back of our head,
But its resilience surfaces soon and continues to escort us in daily life.
It didn't end with the withdraw of troops and the fall of Saigon.

ROCK APES

L ong before the Vietnam War started, there were stories among the people in Southeast Asia of something very strange and enigmatic lurking in the thick, wet, dark, and dense jungles. There were stories passed down of hairy, bipedal, apelike creatures living in troops among the remote regions of the north in the countries of Vietnam, Laos, Cambodia, and Borneo. They were known by various names depending on the regions, but typically names such as *Batutut, Ujit,* and *Nguoi Rung,* all referred to as the *Jungle People.*

The Marines called them *Rock Apes.*

Descriptions vary, but almost always, the apes were described as large, muscular, and covered with long black or reddish-brown hair. They could be aggressive against people and would attack without provocation at times.

As a young Marine heading into Southeast Asia, the stories of rock apes seemed almost too bizarre to be true. *Almost.* There were tons of stories relayed by returning Vietnam veteran Marines, who, in most cases, ended up training the grunts. I always convinced myself that these were stories intended to scare the crap out of you. Nevertheless, I admit there were times when I would be sitting in a hole on perimeter watch, or out on a night ambush in the thick jungle, wondering if it was all bullshit, or whether rock apes were looming. After all, there were still new species being discovered in distant places every year. The Mountain Gorilla wasn't discovered until 1902 in Africa. The most fear-inducing stories came from returning Marines who would speak of rock apes throwing back grenades. At night, around a perimeter especially, if someone heard noises out beyond the wire, it wasn't unusual to throw a fragmentation grenade toward the noise. So, the possibility existed that someone or something could, if fast enough, throw the frag back at you right before it exploded.

I admit, it did cross my mind at times when we weren't sure if there was something probing the wire or not. At that point, you had a choice to make. Toss a frag out there and discourage a *sapper*, or toss a frag out there and chance getting it thrown back in your lap. I typically leaned in the favor of taking my chances and giving it a toss.

Sightings and stories of these creatures weren't limited to the soldiers and Marines. Viet Cong and North Vietnamese Army regulars swore the creatures existed. Supposedly in the early 1970s, two different expeditions were created by the North Vietnamese government to search out and capture or kill one of the creatures. Neither expedition was successful, but that didn't lessen the belief in the rock ape legends.

Personally, I never saw one, nor did anyone I was in the bush with, but that didn't relinquish the fear in the back of your mind that they could be out there.

ELEPHANTS

Elephants have always had a special cultural and religious significance in Vietnam. They are still displayed as architectural ornaments, adorning buildings throughout the country. Currently, the elephant is listed as an endangered species by the government of Vietnam. There has been a long history of elephant trapping and capture there. They have been used more for transportation and beasts of burden, versus the water buffalo that is still used extensively in the rice paddies for cultivation. Today, there is still some limited use of elephants in the lumber industry there, sort of indigenous all-terrain skidders.

During the *American War,* as the Vietnamese call it, elephants were used in transporting supplies, especially down from the north along ancient trails and supply routes. Because of this, elephants became legitimate bombing targets for airstrikes along the various supply routes, most likely drastically reducing their numbers. Even considering the toll from the war, numbers were said to be approximately two thousand wild elephants in 1980. A continuously declining population has resulted in only around 114 in 2000, to nearly zero at the last census in 2004. Today, poaching and loss of habitat from logging are the main cause.

I never saw an elephant while I was in country. While the water buffalo was a relative common sight in the rice paddies, the elephants were not common, at least in the more northern areas where the majority of the Marines were positioned.

There remains another elephant from that era, however. A much larger and deadly and more common elephant than the Asian beast I just mentioned above. This is a beast that can live as long or longer than any wild elephant. You could say it is a beast of burden. This is the proverbial *elephant in the room* during discussions about Vietnam combat veterans and in discussions behind closed doors at countless VA hospitals and clinics across our country. It's an unshakable beast that nearly 30 percent of all combat veterans experience at some level, and for Vietnam veterans following their combat service. Unfortunately, early studies were few, and veterans were simply dismissed as *shell-shocked*, a term left over from WWII and Korea. In the past twenty years, much more is known about the condition. Studies continued with Afghanistan and Iraqi war veterans.

This elephant, of course, is PTSD, *Post-Traumatic Stress Disorder.*

Studies have shown that the veterans who continued to have PTSD decades after their combat experience were found to have considerably more psychological and social problems. They report a lower satisfaction with their marriages, and life in general. They also indicated having a higher divorce rate, parenting problems, and various physical health issues, such as fatigue, aches, colds, and other issues.

It's never easy to admit to such a disorder for fear of being labeled as emotionally unstable. Because of this, the majority of veterans simply try and deal with it themselves. Some do a better job at it than others. Over the years, I slowly admitted to myself that there was a reason why some days I just woke up angry—angry at the world, angry at anyone around me, and even just angry at myself for no apparent reason. In most cases, I was really good at masking these feelings, but part of that would include shutting down to anyone around me. Sometimes even little things would make me angry, things that on other days, I would unknowingly laugh off. Certain people would upset me, but just sometimes. It's never been consistent, which makes it even more difficult to understand. Sometimes walking away would help, but you aren't walking away from the cause, you're just walking away from people—often those who love you most.

Everyone deals with it differently. If you are lucky, you learn what it is and why it's there, giving you a chance at confronting the beast and saving your soul. Too many people never arrive at the chance and can be destroyed. Twenty-two veterans commit suicide every day, according to a recent statistic. That's more than eight thousand veterans a year who can no longer cope with the battle.

I have coped by escaping outside, even just for a short walk. It calms things down. My real relief comes from nature and the quiet and stillness that I absorb in the outdoors. Hunting, fishing, photography, riding an ATV or snowmobile, hiking, or just driving back roads and going nowhere became my salvation, my hope, my reboot. I can feel it coming on in a lot of instances, and knowing when to walk away or what can trigger it is a huge step.

It took a long time to realize that I wasn't a wacky psycho. I was simply struggling with a physiological and psychological reaction to the shit-world that I survived as a nineteen-year-old kid. It was just purely that, a reaction to something totally out of my control, and now it's my body's way of dealing with the aftereffects.

According to a lot of psychologists, replacing bad memories with good memories can help, and continuing to make good memories and experiences is the best therapy for me. Just writing about it, finally, is an enormous relief.

I know this rogue elephant isn't going away, as it has followed me thousands of miles across the world. But because it's a big elephant, it can't hide from me any longer. I'll keep on the lookout and replace it with that big bull elk walking out of the dark timber toward the creek. And I'll keep seeking out those bright meadows and the next undiscovered valley.

THE HUNT II

Fall 1970

I t happens over and over, this recurring dream.

We fly into the drop zone. We find a jungle trail somewhere off the LZ just like all the rest—thick, dark, wet, and quiet. We move out.

Contact is expected from any direction. We finally stop to take a break just as it starts to sprinkle. You could hear distant thunder forecasting another miserable night in the rain. The overcast and rain make it seem ever darker and eerily quiet. That's good and bad. I'm on point that afternoon. I step off the trail and disappear into the curtain of jungle vegetation to keep watch. Despite the wet and cold, I don't like wearing my poncho on patrol because it makes squeaks when you raised your arms. I also hate the way it blocks your hearing. Hearing is all you have in that black-indigo ink darkness. I wait and keep an eye out for any movement or noise.

Suddenly, out of nowhere, a young Viet Cong soldier appears walking down the trail toward me. I wait as my heart and head pound. Then, maybe sensing something isn't right, he stops and looks down the trail. He didn't turn or look back or give a signal, so I think he might be alone. Did this young guerilla soldier see something down the trail? Did he hear my squad? Did one of our guys move too much? They're taking a break. The young VC is going to walk right into them. I can't take a chance. Slowly, I raised my M16 and fire one shot. The man staggers a few steps, then falls forward. I kept looking back down the trail expecting return fire, but nothing. It's dead silent—dark, dead, crazy silence. I slowly turn back and look toward his body as he quivers one last time in the rain. I wait long, anxious minutes that seems like hours.

The quiet is unnerving as the rain stops. I slowly get up and step out onto the trail and gingerly walked toward the lifeless body. My heart feels like it was ready to explode and blow a hole through my flak jacket. I slip my hand under the jacket over my heart to quiet it down. I look down the trail toward the squad, now in their ambush positions like a disciplined rifle squad. I know they have me covered. I kneel and immediately felt the warm pool of blood soak through my jungles to my knees. All is still so quiet. The world stops to observe. I don't know why, but I suddenly reach down and brush the dirt from his face. No remorse, no real feelings, almost a sense of relief. Had I just played God? How was it that at this moment I had total control over the life of another human being?

It slowly happens, incrementally, one contact at a time. I am becoming more of a robot than a human. All that training kicks in. The lifesaving, life-taking training. Robots survive, humans don't. The squad slowly emerges to secure the trail. We pat him down, pull him off the trail, and leave him there. He was young, probably younger than me. As we head back down the trail, it starts raining again. No one celebrates; we just moved on.

I've often wondered who found him.

THE LITTLE GREEN SNAKE
Jungle 1970

I sit there, as still and permanent as the trees and vines beside me—a part of the jungle—moving only my eyes, hoping they didn't give me away. It's too late to move now. I have to take a chance and let nature take its course. *Please let this be another lucky uneventful day.*

Above and to my left, just inches away from my bare sweaty neck, a small shiny green snake sits in the vine next to me, tongue flickering. I'm certain it's a green pit viper. I had seen photos in training and heard all the stories of guys getting bit by this small, innocent looking snake, then dying a slow painful death as its toxic venom swiftly circulates through their helpless body. Strange as it seems, I wasn't really afraid. I was angry at myself for maybe being careless when I sat, for not looking enough. And angry at the snake for being there, right there, right then. I'm angry at this silent killer who, with its deadly strike, releases a toxic venom streaming through the body. As the body reacts and dies a slow death, the snake feels nothing, striking out of instinct, but killing just the same. It neither celebrates nor feels remorse.

I sit there, beside it, wondering if the snake knows I, too, am a killer. I, too, wait for someone to come too close, to come by me. But I am a better and kinder killer. My venom strikes much faster, circulates much quicker, kills much easier, sometimes even without a reaction. I, too, can strike out of instinct, trained instinct, instinct just the same. But the little green snake belongs there. He has adapted over eons, sitting on that vine, sitting right next to my bare neck. We both kill to survive, but he belongs there.

FROM A DISTANCE
1970

Sometimes I would sit in a hole at night and wonder how strange it must be to kill from a distance. To be that B-52 crew thousands of feet in the air above this violent landscape, dropping tons of unbelievable, life-ending carnage out of the airplane. Then flying back to somewhere and having a cold beer in the club. Never witnessing the results, or walking through the burned and ravaged scene.

Or, what was it like to be that Huey or Cobra gunship crew, charging into a fight, unloading thousands of rounds of mini-gun terror into a tree line or rice paddy, and then swiftly disappearing?

Or, the F-4 pilot screaming in out of nowhere, dropping high explosive bombs—or worst yet, napalm—then going vertical and disappearing in seconds.

Did they lie awake at night, and do they still, years later? Can they remember each flight in vivid detail? Or do they?

Why would they, when they have never crawled out of a hole to see who's left, or humped in to take a body count?

And why would they, when they didn't walk through the blood-soaked village, scattered with body parts, trying to find a recognizable clue as to who that used to be?

Do they even know what warm blood smells like?

Had they ever loaded body parts onto a green rubber poncho and prayed they were sending all of him back home?

Had they ever tried to wipe the blood off their hands with jungle leaves, only to discover the leaves were cutting their hands and mixing their blood with blood of the dead?

Why would they, when they haven't walked point and wondered with every step if this was going to be their last?

Why, when they haven't heard the sound of a buddy tripping an invisible wire or trying carefully to step on a leaf, only to pay the ultimate price anyway?

But then, I thank God, they could streak in and out in seconds and not feel the burning heat from their bombs. And I thank God they could just open a hatch thousands of feet in the blue sky and not even see the ordinance fall to the earth, or watch the tracers from their mini-gun rounds race away from their cockpit, like Fourth of July fireworks, to that called in target down there below, somewhere.

Thank God.

I know some will think about it, years later. I hope most don't. Some of us have enough of those thoughts to go around for everyone.

NOT A GOOD DAY TO
BE CHARLIE

Fall 1970

I t could be a scene out of *The King and I*. I'm looking down into
a lush green valley of rice paddies and a quiet little village we
checked out a couple days back on the hump up here. We had just
completed a search-and-destroy a few clicks away and were on our
way back down into the valley. A few days ago, the village had even
offered us some hot rice and water. Now, two skinny water buffalo
are slowly guided along the paddy by young boys, with nothing but a
small leafy branch. The rich wet valley of vibrant green rows of rice,
the bright yellow sunshine, and the rich blue sky—blue that's so blue,
it should be its own primary color.

A few thatched roof huts are scattered along the banks close to
the water. A pot is cooking over the central fire. But I remember the
older woman who stood in the background and avoided eye contact
as I walked by, where everyone else seemed friendly. I remember
seeing a large burn scar on her arm as she smoked her little cigar
looking cigarette.

Now, from up here, I suddenly realize something. As I remember
the hooches and the bamboo roofs, something isn't right. There
weren't any signs of adult men around then, but now I see a couple

eating around the firepit. *Let's not head back down there yet; something just isn't right.*

It suddenly jumps out at me. There is an open hole between the second hut and the firepit, and, sure enough, a trap door that's open. How did we miss that the first time? My peaceful little movie scene now takes on an ominous side, a treacherous side, a dangerous and two-faced side. As we continue to watch, four adults come out of the hole, clad in black silk pajama shorts, each with an AK slung over their shoulder. *Son of a bitch, it's a hostile village after all.* After the warm welcome, the offer of food and water, which no one took, and the perceived friendliness, we now see the apparent false allegiance. They are living for the moment, playing both sides for survival. Another body appears out of the tunnel and hands up a couple small bags of rice to the men already packing up their makeshift backpacks. We are now witnessing a potential large cache of supplies and arms that we probably walked right over a few mornings earlier. I stood just a few feet from the now so obvious tunnel while I reassured the old mamason we are here only to chase VC and protect the village from Charlie. They may have been down in that tunnel all along. We were lucky and blind at the same time.

Our LZ was nearby, so they knew when we landed. We could have walked right into a hornet's nest.

I've seen enough; we call in an airstrike.

Now we wait and watch and listen for the sound of thunder from the sky. Down below, the resupply attempts continue, with more bags handed out of the tunnel. After a few minutes, they close the trap door to the tunnel and drag some branches over the top, then casually call over one of the boys to walk the water buffalo over it, leaving tracks in the dirt so no one would suspect anything. Obviously, it has worked many times before. It had worked flawlessly on us.

They squat around the firepit and begin to drink something and smoke, not in a hurry to leave. Minutes pass by, and just when I begin to wonder where the jets are, there's radio contact from the pilot, and

I hear the distant thunder turn into a roar approaching from behind me, like we instructed the pilot to do. It would be a quick and easy strike. Fly in, drop down into the valley, and run the village. Contact from the pilot again reassures me they are on final approach. There will be no markers down below; the entire village is hostile. The men scramble at the sound of the jets, but by then, it was too late. My mind eases a bit as I realize the two young boys with the buffalo have worked their way to the far side of the rice paddies, far enough from the village to be safe from the airstrike. They will live today—but most likely live to grow a little older and take up arms to fight the poor bastard replacing me. That is the ironic part of it all. Same old thing, I save their life today, only to fight them tomorrow.

If you were lucky, when calling in an airstrike, you would get craft already airborne and looking for a fight. In the area north or west of Da Nang, most likely a Navy or Marine jet was close and on call.

There is nothing like the sound of close combat air support. I still get goose bumps thinking about the F-4 Phantom flying overhead at near treetop level and dropping into the valley below, unleashing a deadly load of five-hundred-pound bombs in a staggered row of fire, shrapnel, and smoke. A second aircraft appeared and mimicked the first run, and that fast, it was over.

The F-4s were long gone before the smoke cleared. And as the hooches burned out, we packed up and headed down to scout and clear the village. We watched a secondary explosion blow a huge crater near the firepit as the tunnel and arms cache detonated, blowing an even larger crater where the VC had been sitting seconds earlier.

Now we will sweep the area to verify kills, gather any information that could be found, and make sure that all the ordinance has exploded and can't be used as a deadly booby trap later.

As I walked through the burning village, a few survivors walked out of the jungle and stared at us as we surveyed the extent of the airstrike. Near the end of the row of the now smoldering black hooches, the same old lady who stood in the background when we first approached the village days before now looked even more worn and tired and angry. She looked away as I made eye contact one last time. She had survived somehow, probably like many times before, as she had known war her entire life. Today, I was the enemy; tomorrow, I may be her friend.

LUCKIEST NIGHT OF
OUR LIVES

Fall 1970

I was attached to two platoons in Mike Company 3rd Battalion, 1st Marine Division after the 7th pulled out of country. It was a strange unit, as we never really saw other platoons in the company, and rarely even the other squads within the platoon. We would be strung out along a resupply route on road security a lot during the days, and ambushes at night. The days of large-scale operations for us were nearing an end in this endless war. It was the ARVN's time to step up and take back their country.

Road security was gravy duty, but boring. It did give us a chance to write letters home and mingle with villagers at times along the roads. I loved giving kids my sweets from the C-Rats, or anything that arrived from home. Most of the time, anything that made it from Minnesota was crushed or spoiled by the time it got there—*if* it got there. Late in the afternoon, the squad leaders would hook up with the platoon commander, typically a young first lieutenant, and get our coordinates for where we were being sent that night. One afternoon, the lieutenant met with me, then a lance corporal, and he had a new guy transferred in from some other unit with him. He wanted me to take him out with my squad that night. I reluctantly agreed, but I hated disrupting our small, tight-knit squad. I brought him back, introduced him to the guys, and told them to get ready to head out.

Our mission for the night was to set up an ambush listening post off a large area of rice paddies a couple clicks or so away from the road. The village was suspected of being friendly to us during the day and friendly with Charlie at night—not that unusual. As we headed out, I stuck the new guy in the middle of the squad and the five of us humped out. I found a viable spot very close to the coordinates passed down, and we set up for the night, the usual, never knowing what to expect.

The routine would be the same. After dark, we take turns staying awake and on watch while the others get some well needed sleep, even though you could hardly ever really call it sleep. I think he had second watch that night, and I was to follow, after his watch, sometime around one in the morning. He would wake me at that time. We settled in, and I made sure he was okay.

I remember opening my eyes and it seemed like it was daylight already. Then it hit me like a brick, and I felt a knot in my chest. No one had awakened me for my watch. I looked toward where the new guy was supposed to be on watch and noticed he was slouched over on his pack. I didn't know if he was dead, but apparently no one had been on watch since he fell asleep or died or whatever. I crawled over to him and grabbed his arm. He was cold and stiff but was still breathing. I woke everyone else, and my radioman recognized the guy had most likely overdosed on something during his watch.

Now that also meant that we were all asleep most of the night out there without anyone keeping watch, something nightmares are made of. An absolute worst-case scenario. I still dream about waking up and finding the squad with all their throats cut and VC sitting around a fire laughing and looking at me—the same dream, over and over, through the years.

I was so upset, I wanted to finish him myself. A couple of the guys were working his arms and legs, trying to revive him and get the blood circulating. I called for a medivac bird to come and get him.

We secured the area for the chopper. As the corpsman was hauling him away on a stretcher, he wanted to know if I knew what was wrong with him. I was so done with the kid, so scared and so pissed at him, I merely said we thought he had malaria-like symptoms and walked away. That next evening, there was contact near that exact location.

Why did the good Lord watch over all of us that night?

Why couldn't I have woken up during the night?

What if we had gotten overrun in our sleep and not had a chance?

Why did I even agree to take him with us that night?

I never knew his name; I never cared what happened to him.

Sometimes I think we should have left him there and said he wandered off during his watch. I don't know if he made it or not, and I really don't care. I'm guessing he most likely got a dishonorable discharge if he was on drugs. I hope so, because that would follow him the rest of his life.

THE BOX

Much has been written about the short- and long-term effects on a person after combat experience. The idea of compartmentalization is one of the explanations of the aftereffects. I think it hits the idea smack on the head, and I've never personally heard a better analogy.

The novel *Matterhorn*, by Karl Marlantes, explains moving through a common compartmentalization progression:

> "Compartmentalization is a critical skill in combat. There simply isn't enough time to deal with all your emotions or feelings while you are in constant conflict with the enemy. When you get really good at it, it is almost like you wield an emotional cleaver. When anything arises that may distract you from the mission, or detract from your combat effectiveness . . . you cut it away.
>
> "Three facts registered simultaneously: the machine gun was silent, Jancowitz was dead, and the opening had to be exploited.
>
> "Due to the high number of inputs at any one moment,

the ability to filter and process only vital information is necessary. Notice his first and last thought involve the tactical situation. He observes the machine guns silence; he orients on the threat and decides it needs to be exploited; and he acts. He establishes fire superiority through accurate suppression, assesses the effectiveness of the suppression, moves to the opening, and kills what needs to be killed.

"Note, the death of his squad leader, whom he loves, registers as a blip devoid of any emotional attachment. I can assure you there are feelings associated with this loss; however, there's just no time to deal with them.

"I can also assure you that these emotions go somewhere. They just don't evaporate into the thin air. Without realizing it, you've packed them into a box, and this ability to cognitively disassociate with the feelings inside that box is what saves you in the heat of the battle.

"At first, maybe you pack a few boxes in the attic. Life is so busy though, and you really don't have time to revisit with any of that stuff, so you end up with a warehouse full of boxes. One day there's a knock at the door, and a few of the boxes are sitting on your front porch. You don't remember requesting any deliveries, and before you can manage to throw them in your garage, they start to unpack themselves. Now, things get messy. The content of the boxes then begin to spill out everywhere, and you're left scrambling to pick up the pieces."

I have never heard or read a more accurate description of the baggage of war. The way he describes it makes an extremely complicated problem seem so simple, but the analogy is so meaningful. It's such a simple analogy, but so spot on.

THE LAND OF
MAKE BELIEVE

Sometimes, in those dark days of war, looking down into a valley
or across a river or scanning a dark tree line became a kind of
hunt. Search-and-destroy patrols were the mission.

Looking for the slightest movement, an out-of-place angle in
the natural vegetation, a puff of smoke from a cigarette. Over time,
I noticed that the young Marines from rural areas—the hunters, the
ridge runners, the hillbilly—all had an edge for seeing the out of
place, the unnatural, the unusual. I would take a ranch kid or a farm
boy any day over a city kid when, in all honesty, lives depended on
it. There just seemed to be a natural or learned instinct and gift to
noticing things, more of an inherent survival skill.

Sometimes, high on a ridge, looking out into that jungle, or across
seemingly endless rice paddies spread out in weird geometric shapes
in a much more random un-geometric green world, I would think
about how, even here in this crazy far off primitive world, man has
changed this mysterious battlefield. What was this place like a hundred
or two hundred years ago? What did it look like before the bomb
craters and napalm and scorched landscapes, before the Chinese, the
French, or the Japanese wreaked havoc and destruction in this rich

and complicated land? Before we left our pock marks and scar tissue on the earth I was looking down upon? If you could remove yourself from the threats and fears and death that lay out there, if given time, would you see a different place? An exotic place of rivers and crude rice paddies, of mountains and primitive peoples, of warm, wet monsoons that nourished a thirsty jade green jungle canopy full of life. Maybe even the cure for cancer is out there, hidden in a simple indigenous little plant that's been there for eons. Why couldn't that elk walk just out from that dark edge and drink from that stream?

But you quickly realize thinking like that can get you killed there.

Wake up. Look for that movement, the odd angle, the wisp of smoke. Stay in the zone; be ready.

THE ANTS AND THE LEAF

Summer 1970

Once while on patrol, we stopped at a small fast flowing stream to fill our canteens. I noticed two large ants floating down the stream, on a large brown leaf. One ant seemed anxious and nervous and kept going back and forth across the leaf and testing the water as if it wanted to get off. The other ant was still and seemed to ride the leaf without fear or concern. Was it too small a space for the first ant? Too risky not knowing where the leaf was headed? All alone? No food? But the one ant wanted to get off. As the leaf floated into a quiet pool, the ant finally crawled off the leaf and began swimming. Suddenly there was a swirl in the water and a small fish rose and consumed the ant. The second ant still lay motionless as the leaf continued to float downstream.

I wondered if it even noticed the first ant and its demise. Could they communicate, and did they? Or was it strictly a case of each ant for himself. Soon, the leaf ran into a stick, and the remaining ant crawled off the leaf and walked across the stick to the bank and headed into the jungle. It seemed strange, but I kept wondering about those ants for the next few hours. Why did they behave so different in this circumstance? I don't think ants have much for brains, at least not like ours. So, was it instinct that drove the behavior? If so, why didn't both ants behave the same? Did each ant have a different survival instinct—one to get out of the danger as fast as possible regardless of risk, the other to ride it out as it was relatively safe and wait until something forced a quick decision? Was the ant that stayed on the leaf—who made it downstream to safety—smarter? But what if by then it was in a foreign territory and was attacked and killed by other aggressive ants? Was that a greater risk?

Every creature at some point may have to make choices and decisions without knowing the outcome. Sometimes the outcome is cast in stone even before the choice is made; that's fate. Sometimes choice determines outcome. Sometimes, a little of both. Are our quick decisions based on a primal instinct? Can we override these quick gut reactions, and reason out the possibilities of the outcome, and then make a more informed decision? Do we, as humans, have an innate, survival mode? Sometimes, due to the specific circumstance, the outcome will be the same no matter what choice we take. Then destiny trumps reason.

Which kind of ant was I? Was time my leaf?

I filled my canteens and moved on along the stream, waiting for my destiny of the day to arrive.

THE BRIDGE

December 19, 1970

O ver fifty-eight thousand men never got a chance to tell this story. I'm one of the lucky ones. I've dreamt this hundreds of times. I've replayed it over in my mind more times than that. It never changes. I've been startled awake during the dream a few times by my wife because I was thrashing around in bed. I feel so guilty when that happens because I don't know what she thinks. I've only told this story to a few people—part of the story.

When I was transferred to Mike Company, and moved to the second platoon, I had volunteered to be the radioman for the squad leader. Eventually, when he was due to go on R&R, I was asked by our lieutenant to take over the squad. It was a tight team of only four Marines, including myself at that point. But I liked that idea.

We had been on road security along a resupply route somewhere west of Da Nang. One afternoon, I was called up by our platoon commander, the lieutenant, to get the coordinates for my squad's night act. We were to set up a night ambush along a trail leading from a village to a large open area of rice paddies—a typical scenario on a typical night, and of late, a typical week, and something I had done countless times. After walking back to the guys, who were lying in the ditch along the road, I studied my map and noticed we were dangerously close to where we had been a few nights before—that fucked-up night when I had to medevac the kid who overdosed and left us without security for most of the night. So, I cursed the dumbass back in the rear somewhere that sent out the coordinates and walked back to the lieutenant to straighten it all out.

Most officers don't appreciate getting second-guessed by anyone, much less a nineteen-year-old enlisted man, even though I had more time in country than he did. I explained that the coordinates were too close to where we had been earlier and there was no way we should go back there this soon, especially when there had been quite the ruckus with the medevac and all. Charlie doesn't miss those things. The lieutenant said I must be looking at it wrong and to get my shit together. Headquarters was never wrong. I invited him to look at the map with me so I could show him the problem. He got pissed, and we had a few choice words, then he ordered me to go back to the squad, gear up, and head out. End of conversation. I walked away shaking my head at the fucked-up world I was in.

At that point, I had a huge choice to make—disobey a direct field order in a combat zone and not go, or do I go, and then set up in a different location? If a chose the latter, no one would know where we were if something were to happen. That would suck, and I just wouldn't do that to the other guys, even though they would have agreed with me. So, we saddled up and headed back out, thinking I would work something out in my head on the way there.

There were only so many ways to get from point A to point B in that maze of dikes and waterways. One of the real issues was a bottleneck in the trails at a bridge crossing a small stream. The bridge was solid and a good place for an ambush by Charlie. With a small squad, the last thing I wanted was to walk into contact. If we made contact, I wanted it on my terms at my choosing. I liked working with a small group, as it was much easier moving around and communicate with each other—very similar to the training conducted in recon school.

As we approached the bridge, I stopped the squad and decided to send the point man up to check it out, to look for trip wires or pressure plates or anything that could trigger a booby trap. The bridge was a small concrete arch without sides. We set up to cover him in case all hell broke loose. I told him, if the shit hits the fan, don't jump in the water, because who knows what they could have hidden in there. Just try and use the bridge for cover and roll back down off the arch toward us.

We covered him as he slowly approached the bridge, and I waited with my guts in my throat and heart pounding under my flak jacket. I knew he was a good point man, a ridge runner from West Virginia or somewhere, and very woods wise. As he stepped up onto the concrete and began to slowly start across, I was playing out in my mind what we would do if he took fire, and how we would try and suppress it, allowing him to get back off the bridge. Textbook fire team reaction. The only problem is a textbook squad has three fire teams with three or four marines in each team. And we had only four Marines total. But we would adapt and conquer to survive.

He got across the arch and on to the trail on the other side, took a knee, and motioned us forward as he scoured the nearby tree line. I got up and started to approach the bridge with my radioman, who was within an arm's reach like he was supposed to be. I knew that I was the probable target if something was going to happen, because by knocking out the squad leader and his radioman, the rest of the squad would be left without direction, and that was Charlie's MO—sort of Guerilla Warfare 101, and they used this tactic whenever possible.

I cautiously continued up the arch of the bridge and crested the top. Suddenly it was if an F-4 had ignited its engines directly in front of me. A wall of intense heat hit me like a blast furnace and sucked the air out of my lungs. That's what I remember the most, the intense heat and bright, blinding ball of fire. A shock wave slammed my head as if my brain exploded. Everything slowed as if even time itself waited to see what was going to happen next. I was thrown back and hit the deck of the bridge hard, and as I looked up at the sky, all I could see was dark smoke. I'm not sure when I realized what had happened, but I remember instinctively reaching up for my helmet, and it was gone. I struggled to take a deep breath, while frantically reaching around for my rifle. I glanced to my left, and my radioman was on the deck and also hit, and I began grabbing for the handset of the radio to call for backup. I remember yelling, "Don't roll into the water. We've got to get off the bridge!" As I went to grab the radio handset, I felt for my rifle, but I couldn't grip it because my arm was numb. Everything was muffled, and I could barely hear the firefight. I struggled to breathe. Reaching for the handset with my other hand, I tried to contact the platoon leader. Finally, someone came on the net, and I told them we had been hit and requested backup and support and a medevac chopper. I was trying to evaluate our situation and whether anyone else was hit. I realized it was getting dark, which would be our friend. I knew I was bleeding bad. A side of me just wanted us all to be able to hide in the dark and wait for support. I could overhear the platoon commander on the radio. As I rolled over to the other side of the bridge, small arms rounds started to hit the bridge deck in front and to the side of me. I remember the smell of cement dust as the AK rounds jackhammered the deck up and edged closer to me. It's called *walking the dog* in training. You observe where your rounds are hitting and walk the rounds right up to your target. Suddenly something ripped through my hand, and I looked down and half of my hand was hanging down like a broken branch, split open by the rounds. I was bleeding profusely from my legs and groin as well and could see blood pulsing from my thigh through my torn jungles. I knew I had to stuff something down there to stop the bleeding. I had a first aid pack somewhere in the pockets of my flak jacket, but when I reached to get it, all I could feel was sharp shrapnel imbedded across the front of the jacket. I remembered I had a gauze pack in the cargo pocket and stuffed it between my legs. My radioman was quiet, and as I tried to see if I could crawl around to check on him, the sky lit up. I looked up and saw a large bright yellow flare floating across the sky like a child's balloon and casting lethal light across the entire area around the bridge. I lay there exposed, but I don't remember taking fire after that. What I next remember is speaking over the radio to the pilot of the medevac bird who wanted to know if we were still taking fire, and if an LZ was secure. I remember yelling at him that I had no one to set up a secure LZ and to just land that fucking bird. Then I heard and saw a gunship fly overhead and open up on the tree line. At some point, a squad or two from our platoon must have arrived to secure the LZ. When I saw the gunship, I can remember laying my head down on the bridge and feeling the blood oozing out of my body and thinking, *Maybe this isn't a bad way to die.* I still had no pain; how could I? Maybe I was already dead and my body was simply bleeding out and soaking into the concrete. I could just evaporate into the warm, wet, humid air and be gone. I'd be out of this shithole. I would just be a bloodstain etched forever into a shitty little concrete bridge, beside a bunch of stinking little rice paddies, near an unfriendly village a world away from everything I loved. A big blood stain that maybe the monsoons would eventually wash off and that scorching sun would fade away.

What if that was it? I never imagined dying over there, which is how my nineteen-year mind worked. But here I was, on my way out. No more girlfriends, no wife, no family, no more mountains and fields and woods. *Now what? Did that cobra kick ass in the tree line? Should I pray? Maybe I should take my chances and go against my gut and just roll into the stream and float away.*

The upside to death would be no more humping, no more jungle, no more stinky rice patties, no more insects, snakes, parasites, jock rash, diarrhea, and gooks! *Should I stop the bleeding? Or does it even matter anymore?*

Suddenly my nose burned and I started to cough. *Is this where I cough up blood and die like in the war movies? Choke on my own blood?* I realized that it was jet engine exhaust that was choking me, and a chopper must be landing. I remember someone suddenly kneeling over me and talking. I could see his lips moving, but I couldn't hear him. Then they lifted me up onto a stretcher. As my soul floated up, I was literally watching from above as I lay on the stretcher on that little shitty bridge, and as they began to carry me into the waiting chopper. There were no lights, but the ground was bright. There was no sound, but suddenly I could hear my thoughts. There were few around, except everyone was there now. There was no smell, but I could see the fumes. Was it me they were carrying? *Am I dead? Where is everyone else? Where are Herbie and Fat Balls and JR?* I wanted to help carry the stretcher like I had done before, but I was somehow content to just watch myself leave—have them take me away.

Am I inside the bird? I hope so. Get me off this bridge. Was I wrapped up in a poncho? I watched as the chopper lifted off. Then I closed my eyes.

THE LAST HELICOPTER

There was a saying over there. "You never want to be on the first bird in or the last bird out." Unless they have gunship escorts, the first bird in tests the waters and usually hits the shit. The last bird out is usually in a big hurry, and even if Charlie is laying low, or just got his ass kicked, he can't resist a parting shot at the last bird out.

All of a sudden, I was on a last bird out, even though I didn't realize it at the time. I was headed back to somewhere slightly less chaotic and dangerous than where I had just been. As for the platoon, I imagine they just watched the bird leave, picked up their shit, and headed back out. I was told much later on that the company swept the village near the site, but I don't know for sure what happened after that.

It's often said that the first hour after you're hit is the most critical one on the battlefield. Most injured guys die within that first hour, most of them bleeding out. It's when the Grim Reaper stands over you and has to decide, "Should I waste my time here or move on to an easier score?" Maybe that's why, for those guys, time stands still. I felt it that night. Time slows to a stop and waits, like it did for me. It waits to see if you have what it takes to pull through the shit. Then, when it's satisfied, it moves on. Maybe time is the Grim Reaper.

Corpsman in the field, and the crew that lands with the medevac bird, help get you through that first hour. They are the hands of God—the hands that work on you, pound on you, stick needles in you, and if you're lucky, really lucky, the hands that hold your hand and reassure you that everything is going to be fine, whether it really is or not. Or hold your hand, and introduce you to your God. I wish I knew or could have met those guys on the chopper that night. I have no memories of being on that bird, only of watching myself be carried into the chopper. I would love to meet those who got me through that first hour, and the medical staff at First Med in Da Nang. I truly would love to thank them for giving me fifty extra years to try and do something with my life.

That was my last helicopter ride, the ride from the bridge that night. I didn't have to worry about the stories you hear about the marine who gets shot down on the last ride from the bush; we made it out.

I remember wondering sometimes, alone at night in a hastily dug hole somewhere, what it would be like jumping aboard a Huey or hopping on a supply bird for that last chopper ride in from the bush. Securing from the bush was what we all waited for. I'm guessing a lot of guys wondered about that same thing. Those were good thoughts to have. And you cherished good thoughts in those days.

But good thoughts were expensive and could be dangerous. Sometimes I couldn't help but think about how majestic that big bull elk was along Timber Creek that evening in the national park—the muted browns and blacks and tans of his hide, the dark antlers with snow white tips, the green and grey pieces of bark clinging to his rack from rubbing on a sapling. The black-green dark timber backdrop, the mesmerizing sound of the water flowing over the rocks in the stream, and the darkening blue-grey sky of evening, a sliver of a hint of the early fall moon—it was such a simple memory, but such a lasting one. I close my eyes today and see the same clear picture.

He was most likely a herd bull. A dominant breeding bull, so also a warrior. Those thoughts took me to a happy place, memories that counteract, at least for a moment, the hurt and fright of war.

Sometimes I still think and feel like I got robbed of that last ride out. I never got to feel that nervous tension and that elated, cautious, joyous feeling flying back to Da Nang—knowing it was for the last time, spotting the South China Sea and the sprawling airbase next to it. I never got to head back to the armory and hand in my M16. I guess it doesn't really matter. After all, I got my ride back, and probably a lot faster than I would have had I been on a resupply bird. I just didn't know it at the time. And maybe someone was holding my hand.

My records show that I was flown from the bush to 1st Medical Battalion in Da Nang, RVN. I was apparently there for four days, stabilized, then flown to the hospital at Marine Corps Base, Camp Butler, Yoko, Japan. It was there, and at some time during the nine days that followed, I apparently spoke on the phone with my oldest brother, who somehow tracked me down through the USO or the Red Cross, I'm guessing. I don't recall much about that conversation; I wish I did. He told me about it a few years later, over a beer in a fishing boat.

On New Year's Eve, Thursday, December 31, 1970, I was loaded onto a C-141 Medical evacuation jet and flown back to the world. It was at some point in time during that flight, that off and on, things started to come around. I can remember lifting my head up from the bed and seeing this huge open plane full of beds and cots. I remember walking, wounded. I don't remember the first thing anyone said to me. I hope they said, "Hey, you're on your way home, Marine!"

I really wish I remembered that too. Those would have been the good memories.

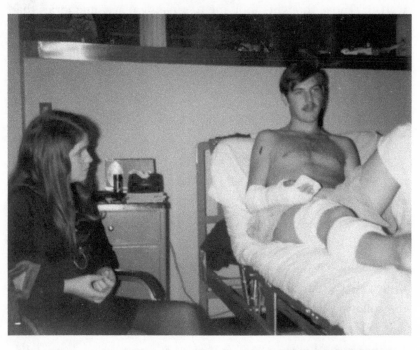

COLLEGE

1971-1975

On June 4, I received my official honorable and medical discharge from the Marine Corps. I had spent the last six months at various military hospitals, from Da Nang to Camp Butler in Japan, to Great Lakes Naval Hospital, near Chicago. The last few weeks at Great Lakes, I was finally allowed to drive back and forth to home in Minnesota for weekends. I bought a 1970 Opel GT my first trip back home, and drove it while awaiting the findings of the medical board.

When I got back for good, I registered for fall semester at the local junior college. I was financially set. Because of my service-related disability, I would receive the full GI Bill, plus vocational rehab benefits, as long as I stayed in school. That was a tremendous help in laying out my future plans.

The first couple years went by in a blur. That first summer, I was home back on Mom and Dad's little farm. I had gotten married my sophomore year and was a father by the end of that year.

The birth of my first son, Paul, was the greatest thing I had ever experienced. It was also one of the most stabilizing things that could have happened at the time. I couldn't wait to be able to teach him to hunt and fish and camp and track wild critters. I think it grounded me and gave me a real reason to tough it out in school. Besides, my dream of becoming a game warden was becoming a bit more real.

College was emotionally hard. I knew I was a good student in high school, and learning was easy for me, but it was more challenging—taking eighteen- to twenty-two credits per semester so that I could graduate faster. That, with being newly married and a new dad, seemed overwhelming at times. After my first year of college, I started to realize that the college campus could be a very cold and lonely place for a Vietnam veteran. By the time I transferred to the College of Natural Resources in Stevens Point Wisconsin, I was really struggling emotionally. Maybe I should have just packed up and moved the family to Alaska. Instead, we moved from Minnesota to Wisconsin and into a mobile home park outside of town. It seemed to help being able to leave the campus and drive out of town those few miles into the woods. That wooded park was filled with other married college students, and some were even veterans.

Going to college, back from Vietnam at age twenty, and being married with a child was not untypical in the trailer park. It beat living in town. There were a couple veterans living there that I was naturally drawn to, which helped a lot. The problem was, they weren't combat vets, and they didn't have the baggage that comes with that—the dreams, the flashbacks, the long and lonely periods of guilt and confusion, mixed with an enormous inner pride that I feel for having lived through it all, and just being a proud Marine.

I joined the vets club on campus, but that didn't really help. I didn't need to hear a bunch of bullshit war stories. My salvation would be walks in the woods—and the few times I could go out and sit in a bow stand alone and sort through things in my head. I would always feel guilty if I studied instead of spending time with my family, but I couldn't get through the tough science curriculum without doing so.

Sometimes I thought of quitting school, but I couldn't live with myself if I quit; I had made a promise to myself to keep trying. All those nights in training and the long days and longer nights in the bush, I had promised myself, *If I just get through this I'll get back and go to college and be set.* I somehow managed to get through by just listening in class, taking notes, and retaining enough information to pass the courses. I had no real involvement on campus except to go to class and leave. I kept to myself and slipped through college getting Bs and Cs without mentally or emotionally being there. I recall having to complete an off-campus summer camp in Northern Wisconsin as part of the requirements for the wildlife and natural resources degree. For four weeks, I was away from my family, the real only stability I had. Part of the course was memorizing various species of plants, which I took some enjoyment from. But I remember the day of the final test for that class. We walked down a path through the woods to identify all the various plants that were marked. I recall walking along and my thoughts careening away from the taxonomy of plants to thinking about where Charlie would be hiding, or where the best place to set up an ambush would be. I suddenly looked down near the end of the walk and realized that I had left a good share of the test sheet blank as I had been walking through another world.

I had to temporarily drop out the last semester of my junior year to have more surgery on my hand, so my graduation was delayed almost six months. Early in my senior year, we had a beautiful daughter, Angela, and we were now a family of four. Taking the kids outside on walks and to fish, and just driving around and looking for wildlife, was great therapy for me, and the kids seemed to love it too. Meanwhile, during all this, our marriage just sort of limped along.

Winter of my senior year, I had applied for a game warden position in the state of Minnesota—my lifelong dream and promise to myself when I enlisted. Those opportunities were few and far between, as budgets were tight, but Minnesota was going to hire two new officer candidates. It was an exhaustive procedure, involving written exams, oral interviews, and physical tests on strength and agility. I thrived and completed each phase. But what made it all but impossible was that both the federal and state hiring mandates required certain quotas to meet the Equal Opportunity Act minimums. In other words, there was little chance in 1975 that a white male would fulfill the imposed restrictions set by the new employment laws. I was somewhat aware of this but didn't realize the ramifications at the state Department of Natural Resource level. I made the final top-ten candidates and drove to St. Paul for a final oral interview in front of a board, and took another lengthy final written exam. I just had to hope that my veteran's status would help push me through. Two weeks later, I got a call from a training supervisor to let me know I was selected as one of the two candidates; maybe the mandatory veteran's preference points got me through. Needless to say, I was ecstatic. I was on top of the world. The plan was beginning to finally seem within my grasp. Shortly after this, I met with my potential supervisor at the farm to set up a training schedule—starting after my graduation from college that year.

I can't describe the high I was on. All my work and dreams—and one of the reasons I enlisted in the Marine Corps—were about to pay off for me. I had a great evening meeting with him as we planned for the next six months. They wanted me to graduate as I was only one semester away. But—

At the end of the night, while we were standing in the back entry of the farmhouse, and while the officer was putting on his coat, I mentioned that I wasn't sure if my eye would have kept me out of the program. He stopped and looked over at me and said, "What do you mean, your eye?" I immediately knew I had blown it. My heart sank and my chest got tight, like when I walked point. I told him that I had lost my eye in Vietnam and that my left eye was a prosthetic.

Somehow, someway, after all the tests, all the physical exams and records they had procured over the last three months, they had missed that detail in my VA medical records. And during the physical exam with their doctors, they never isolated each eye during the eye exam.

He came back inside and sat down at the kitchen table in disbelief. Because it was a law enforcement job, the vision handicap would be a

of the back forty. There are four more houses back there, sprawling across that little field where I watched the buck come and go in the tall green cornstalks and soft fragrant hay meadows. The new ground cover came trucked in on pallets and was unrolled as Bermuda, fescue, and Kentucky grass instead of the sweet clover, alfalfa, and timothy that once grew deep-rooted and strong and nitrogen-fixing. The maples, oaks, and pines have been mostly replaced with Russian olive, hybrid poplar, Chinese elm, and clump birch. The cottontails and woodchucks no longer nest in fallen logs and brush piles and holes in the field, instead taking modern homes in window wells and culverts and under plastic garden sheds and composite decking.

I still have the old Ford tractor that Dad gave me when they moved off the farm and into town. We moved out there immediately. He never formally passed it on to me, but said something like "It just belongs here." Years later, after he passed, I found a handwritten bill of sale on white theme paper among the contents of his desk that were dropped into a box to be looked at later. The official document. That little gray tractor that I first learned to drive on, and eagerly mowed thistles in the pasture, and raked hay into neat wonderfully smelling windrows, still sits tucked away inside my garage up in the north woods. I sold it once, and it broke my heart. I eventually bought it back after years of searching, thanks to my wonderfully understanding and determined wife. I'll never get rid of it again.

The guilt of leaving that little farm still eats at me. Whenever we go back to that area, I always drive by, even though, had it not been for the barn and hardly recognizable relocated house, you would never really know it once was a farm. It's hard not to tear up when passing by; so rarely do I slow down.

In the course of saving myself, I lost that part of myself—that special warm and nurturing rearing pond of my youth, my sanctuary later in life. Yes, the land is still there, but like so many farms, the soul of the land is forever gone. Yet, had I stayed there, the past decades wouldn't be what they were—my life.

THE CABIN

1978

"Sometimes logs can build much more than a cabin."

—FF

After college and my devastating disqualification by the state of Minnesota, I trudged along in a career with my then in-laws back in Minnesota. It was a sometimes challenging job with good money but no life. My salvation was the family and spending as much time outdoors as I could.

In the summer of 1978, we purchased forty acres of woods in northern Wisconsin. We would drive up as a family and camp and fish in the nearby lakes and streams and explore the acres and acres of public county forest all around. I wanted the kids to feel as at home in the woods as I had growing up. I wanted this to be our little family's special place. Sometimes I would head up alone and camp and walk the woods all day with no real agenda except to be alone and to start to find myself again. I started to deer hunt again.

My brother lived twenty minutes from the property, and we would spend time together exploring the area and getting to know each other as adults. I never remembered my two older brothers, as they had gone away to college when I was still pretty young. It was great hanging out, snowmobiling, fishing, and riding ATVs with my brother. There were also times when, somehow, he knew I needed time alone, and he respected that.

The following year, I decided to build a log cabin on the property. In 1979, I purchased the logs and lumber from a small local sawmill that sold do-it-yourself cabin packages. I think it was the do-it-yourself-part that really interested me.

Some weeks later, two semitrucks worked their way down the sandy, two-track county forest trail and onto the forty, and up to the waiting concrete slab. We unloaded over 150 logs, all cut, mortised, and splined, and large black irons to connect the beams, rough sawed window and door frames, logs for the stairway, slab doors, 256 pieces of 2x6x16-foot tongue-and-grooved pine decking, fifty pounds of 20D spikes, and a crate of bolts and nuts and metal rods. What a gorgeous sight. Therapy, by way of flatbed trucks.

The next couple days, my brother and I sorted all the logs by length to make it easier to follow the plans as we got ready to start building the cabin. My brother helped when he could; he was still teaching, and I spent every spare minute I could up there on the pine- and aspen-covered forty. I don't know if I knew it at the time, but with each log, I was not only building our little cabin, but I was rebuilding my life, day by day, log by log, course by course. Physically, emotionally, and mentally healing back.

When the log walls were up and I had decked over the future loft area, I would sleep up on the loft deck in the open. I would often wake up during the starlit night and stare at the constellations. I slowly began to appreciate the darkness of the night again, to listen to the night sounds and relax to their music. The wild was ever so slowly beginning to come back and renew my life. I still slept with a pistol close by, though.

One early morning, I awoke predawn to the muted growls of my Great Pyrenees lying beside me up on the loft. I rolled over in my sleeping bag and realized he was watching a bobcat in a tree just a few feet off the edge of the loft decking. The three of us spent the next ten or fifteen minutes, lying almost eye-to-eye, a few feet apart, staring at each other. However, it seemed relaxed. When the dog sensed we weren't threatened by the bobcat, he calmed down. It was a mutual stand-off; there was no peace accord, no treaty, no needed cease-fire. Just the bobcat, the dog and me, watching and observing and studying each other. I eventually dozed back off, and when I woke up later, the dog was still on guard, but the bobcat was gone from the tree. Both the bobcat and the dog are long a part of the forest soils now, but I still have that special memory, and I wonder how long they remembered that early summer morning.

Building the peaks and loft walls were challenging. With little equipment up there, it got crazy a time or two lifting twenty-foot logs up and onto the support beams and purlins. Standing on the top of a ten-foot step ladder, on top of a kitchen table, and thrusting the log up in one fluid motion seemed to work just fine. Both my brother and I survived.

I finished the cabin that fall before it got too cold. I ordered a new Vermont Castings wood stove to warm the cold winter nights and cool, rainy summer days. The stove is still in the cabin, after countless fires and soothing therapy sessions. It shipped directly from the factory in Vermont, on a pallet that I had delivered to my brother's house, because the delivery truck wouldn't drive into the woods. We grunted it up to the cabin and skidded it into place in the center of the cabin. It has burned through cords and cords of firewood. I remember the first fire in it, smelling the paint burning off the chimney pipes, and the new cast iron popping as the heat rose inside for the first time. That old stove and I are both well seasoned now, having mulled a lot of things over forty-some years. It keeps a good secret, and never judges you no matter how mixed up and crazy the conversation gets. It has given me years of warmth and security and comfort, sometimes when nothing else could. It is hard and cold as iron, as I am at times, but with a little effort, it will warm up and comfort you, as long as you keep watching and listening. Time goes on and the cabin has some cracks and splits, it has settled a bit, and there is moss on the logs. The roof has been repaired once, and it needs to be scraped and re-stained—just like me. But we are both still weathertight, strong, and steady. When my time comes, and the Creator makes that call, if I can't pass up here at the lake, I hope I can be at that simple little log cabin, on the forty, in those jack pine woods. I could easily slip away knowing that the little cast-iron stove from Vermont will live on. And that's the way it should be.

MITCHELL LAKE

The 1980s and 90s

Life moved along at a steady pace. It doesn't wait for anyone. Work was busy and challenging. We had another daughter, Christy, and another son, Michael, and were now a family of six. I still loved being a dad and watching the kids grow and start to become their individual little selves. I wanted to spend every spare moment at the cabin in the woods, but our busy lives prevented most of that. The kids loved to go to the cabin too, but got involved in school activities and sports, and time slipped away. The stresses at work and at home would continue to keep aggravating the underlying feelings of loneliness, anger, and hopelessness. I felt like I was a ticking time bomb, a grenade with the pin already pulled and ready to be tossed through the air. My short trips to the cabin, a few fishing trips and hunting in the fall, were what I looked forward to the most. I would count down the days before each deer season or fishing season. It seemed like the rest of my life was just there and existing, despite it all. My kids were the best distraction in the daily routine.

In the mid-eighties, my wife and I got divorced. We were just two completely different people. We had joint custody of the kids, but they lived mostly with their mom. I looked forward to the weekends that we could be together and do things. Those next few years were focused on my kids, keeping my head straight, and dreaming about changing my career and escaping up north to the woods. I fished more, I hunted more, and I relaxed a bit more. It was the right change. It became clear—the more I was out in nature, the more relaxed and secure I felt. I continued to work the same job in the construction field, for four more years, but I decided I needed to have a game plan.

I had gone into the Boundary Waters in my boy scouting days and always remembered the wild, open, lake—the water, the rocky shorelines, the wildlife, and the solitude. To me, the call of the wild was a wolf howl and a loon call. Nowhere did I feel more a part of the natural world than when I would hear those luring calls. I soon decided that I would pick up and move to extreme northern Minnesota. Most of the wolf studies I had been reading took place there, so I focused on two areas close to the Boundary Waters Wilderness Area—prime wolf country. I decided to look for a small lodge or resort and take a stab at living that life. So, for over a year in the late eighties, I researched and visited countless potential lodges in the Ely area and the Grand Marias area. It would still only be about a half a day's drive from the kids. I had made my mind up; it was going to be either in the Ely area, or further east up the Gunflint Trail, both on the edge of the wilderness. I had camped and fished the areas to some extent, but this would be nothing like that. I was going to jump in with both feet and make the move, get out of Dodge—take the leap into the wild!

In the early winter of 1990-91, I left Rochester and drove 326 miles north to the end of a township road to where the snowplow had stopped and turned around. It was a snowy start to winter with deep snow covering everything around me as I got out of the car and pulled on my boots. My destination was a cozy resort, then closed for the winter, that was listed for sale approximately four-and-a-half miles from Ely, Minnesota. The photos the real estate agent had sent to me looked promising, but I had been down that mental road before, and I realized that photos can be very deceiving. But I was excited as I drove to the area. My heart was pounding, but in a good way this time.

It was a tough walk in that last half mile or so through the deep snow, and by the time I got to the lodge, I was sweating profusely. It was mid-afternoon, and dark came fast in the winter, so I needed to move as fast as I could to check things out. The main door of the lodge was unlocked—a good sign! I put my shoulder to the door to coax it open and walked into yesteryear. It smelled like every old log lodge that I had ever experienced—sort of a combination of wood, varnish, pine, dust, and stale smoke, but one of the most welcoming and natural smells I had experienced in a long time.

I began to walk around, finding light switch after light switch, each one spotlighting a magical authentic north woods stage. It was as if someone hijacked my dreams of what I had imagined for years and staged it all right in front of me as the curtain rose in a one-act play. I was standing at the edge of the stage, taking it all in. *Could this be home?* I suddenly realized that I needed to keep looking around the place and walked out of the lodge toward one of the cabins closer to the frozen, snow-covered lake. A vast, windswept wilderness lay in front of me as I slowly and meticulously followed the shoreline with my eyes as far as I could see—the dead of winter in lake country. It was mythical and real at the same time.

I had time to look into two of the log cabins before it got dark. As the sun hit the horizon, I walked toward the lake and stood there listening to *nothing*. Before me was a cold and white unforgiving wildland that drew me in deeper the longer I stood there. I was captured by the primitive landscape of winter. *Could there possibly be a more peaceful spot on this earth?* I felt warm in the cold, safe in the growing darkness, and an unexplained peace in my soul. It softly and gently took my hand and pulled me away from that violent place on the other side of the world, that haunting place I could never really escape from—until that moment. I was home!

On my walk back out, I noticed a depression in the snow over my boot prints. Coming in from the side were a set of what appeared to be large dog tracks, but I knew they weren't dog tracks. Wolf tracks, and I had been there less than an hour!

I don't think I slept that night back in Ely at the motel. I kept closing my eyes and seeing the warm brown hues of the logs, and the snowy wintery look of the cabins by the lake. It was like a Terry Redlin painting, and I wanted to be sitting in one of the cabins by the window where he always had rays of light radiating out and illuminating the ground next to it.

I called the agent that evening from the motel and told him the search was over and I wanted to make an offer as soon as possible. It was his exclusive listing, so he said I was safe, he would mail me the purchase agreement, and we could execute it over the phone the next day. It was actually two days of anxious torture before the large envelope came in the mail. I read it over, signed it, and mailed it back that same day.

The next couple weeks meant more waiting and unnerving days between phone calls from the agent. There were a few details to work through, but it sounded encouraging, yet not final.

One of the next weekends, I drove back up with my daughter Angela and spent the day walking around the resort with a video camera, looking over inventory and all the complicated details of purchasing a property and a business. My daughter was the first one to see it, and I remember her laughing and saying that I was crazy, but she absolutely loved it.

It was in early February that I signed on the dotted line and closed on the resort. I had just purchased a lodge with a small restaurant and bar, seventeen cabins, thirty-three acres of boreal forest, and almost a half mile of shoreline on Mitchell Lake, in the Superior National Forest, at the end of the road in extreme northern Minnesota. I realized later that I had purchased the property without ever seeing the shoreline and lake unfrozen. But that could be my wonderful reward and surprise in the spring.

I gave my notice at work, and in March 1991, I began spending time back and forth between the farm and the resort, getting ready for the final big move. It was a day of mixed emotions as I drove out of the driveway of the farm and headed north. That farm had been my world, my support group, my refuge for so long, and now I was leaving it—leaving the security of the place I felt comfortable in and sought solace in, where for all practical purposes, I was raised on. But I had to look ahead.

I will never forget the first day that I woke and realized the lake had opened. It was late March and ice-out was official, and I immediately ran down to the beach and stood in awe as I soaked in the tranquility and beauty of Mitchell Lake and the Superior National Forest shoreline around it. This was now my home.

Everyone I knew told me that it would be a work farm and a money pit. There was an unbelievable amount of work to be done before the first guests would arrive in May for fishing season. All the cabins needed work, but I made a list of priorities and began checking off things I completed. It was a work farm, as some people called it, and I absolutely thrived on it. I was outside nearly all day while the resort didn't have guests yet, and nearly outside all day even when there were guests. I moved into the upstairs of the lodge, and I don't think I ever closed the windows that summer for fear of missing the loon call or wolf howls.

The immediate area was home to moose, deer, bear, bobcat, an occasional lynx, otter, wolves, mink, marten, fox, fisher, and tons of waterfowl, and loons right outside my windows. In a matter of a few weeks, it felt like I had been there forever. The wildlife and natural resource biologist in me came back in a flash. I was the owner, the janitor, the maintenance man, the cook, the bartender, the bait shop guy, the dock boy, but most of all, the naturalist. I was back in my element, out in nature in one of the largest national forests in the country. At age thirty-nine, I was as happy as I had been since high school.

Those dark memories and thoughts and nightmares of war never really go away. But when the light shines bright in between those bad times, they don't seem as dark. I knew the dark haunting memories could never just disappear, but I could finally accept that and make the most of the other times. I would step aside and try and *watch the battle* instead of being in the battle. Thank the good Lord for all the bright days and the grace and strength to push through the bad days. It was a never-ending war, but all wars are never-ending. We never seem to realize that, when it starts, it will never end for those who go to war. But the human spirit is strong and resilient and will help you confront that never-ending war with you.

On December 6, 1991, I married my soul mate. I didn't fully realize it at the time, but she would be the brightest light entering my life—a light that never goes out, a strength that shames mine, a love that encompasses the true meaning of that emotion, and a partner in all I do and all I am.

Yes, 1991 goes down as my favorite year of all!

LIFE AT THE END OF THE ROAD

Summer of 1991

My first summer on Mitchell Lake was crazy, fun, hard, challenging, and a bit lonely. I know it seems crazy that one could be lonely when there are a lot of people around, but sometimes it can actually make you feel alone. I was swamped with things to do, so time went by fast. Heather and I weren't married yet, and she was still five and a half hours away in southern Minnesota. She would come up most of the weekends to help, only to drive back late Sunday night, leaving a huge void in my heart. I felt bad, but we loved being together up there, and I couldn't leave. It was a summer of new challenges—running the lodge and preparing for our wedding in December. Thanks to help from Heather, friends, relatives, my kids, and a new fresh outlook on life, we made it through. The lodge was a community, and we met new friends who had been coming up to Mitchell Lake for decades as well as new clients from our advertising campaigns. I was now living in the wild on the lake, and the healing power of the place was tremendous, comforting, and all around me.

That first fall was quiet at the lodge, which was a double-edged sword. It was peaceful to have the place to myself after a hectic first season, but at the same time, I was lonely when everyone was gone. Heather would still come up most weekends, but I remember feeling extremely alone when I would watch her drive out to go back south on Sundays. Had I not been where I was, in the natural surroundings of Mitchell Lake and Superior National Forest, it might have been too much at the time.

I spent that deer season hunting at the lodge and at the cabin in Wisconsin with my son, brother, and nephew, and after that, I immediately drove down to Rochester to make final preparations for the wedding. On December 6, 1991, Heather and I were married in a beautiful ceremony at the Mayo Estate outside of Rochester. The next afternoon, we flew to Hawaii for our honeymoon. A couple weeks later, we flew back and drove up to our new home together at the lodge.

Heather wasn't the big woods person I was, and we knew it would be an adjustment for her to be suddenly living twelve miles from the Canadian border on a lake in the dead of winter—all while adjusting to life as a new bride, too.

I was still figuring the place out after spending the first summer and fall on the lake. I knew that the lodge that would be our home needed some work, but somewhat to my surprise, we returned from our honeymoon to frozen pipes, no running water, and a cold lodge. I remember Heather waking up cold the first morning back and saying, "The adventure begins today!"

If I remember right, it took me a few days of torches, heaters, and a rented steamer to get everything thawed and flowing again. We immediately added a large cast-iron wood stove in the lodge, just like the one at the cabin, and kept it going 24/7. Our life in the north woods together had begun. Maybe I'll write a separate book someday on the adventure at the resort, but suffice it to say, it was everything we imagined it would be and everything we couldn't even imagine! But I was with my soul mate in the wild, and that is all that mattered.

The wilds of Mitchell Lake would nurture us as a couple and

continue to heal my spirit and soul. I now had the love of nature and the love of my life in one unbelievable place. I knew I was so lucky.

When we sold the resort years later, we knew we were going to stay in the area, but we never expected to find a home as quiet and peaceful as Mitchell Lake had been for us. It took over a year, but as fate would have it, an adjacent neighbor at the lodge decided to sell his property, and we were able to again purchase our own little private haven on Mitchell Lake. It was a beautiful piece of property of fifteen acres and nine hundred feet of shoreline on the lake. Along with it came a garage and a mobile home that we moved into. I laughed as I remembered telling Heather that I had come full circle. I lived in a mobile home in college; now, years later, I was back in a mobile home again. But it was paradise. We settled in, and before I knew it, I accepted a job with the Nature Conservancy in Colorado. So, for the next four years, Mitchell Lake would be our "lake place" in Minnesota until we moved back for good.

COLORADO AGAIN

March 2000

I believe in fate, with perhaps a bit of divine intervention from the Creator.

Life takes strange twists and turns sometimes. My first trip to the mountains in 1969, before I enlisted in the Marines, was one of the most unforgettable experiences in my life, in a good way. Thirty years later, we are moving out to Colorado, just for a few years, to a large valley surrounded by fourteen-thousand-foot peaks of the Rockies, to live there and work for the Nature Conservancy. If there was ever a job description that was created to fit my background, this was it.

The Nature Conservancy had just recently purchased a large ranch in the heart of the San Luis Valley in southern Colorado, adjacent to the Great Sand Dunes National Monument (now a National Park). Before we take on the reasons for the purchase, we need to look at the physical and geographical makeup of this unique valley.

The San Luis Valley is the only desert in Colorado, but it sits on top of billions of acre-feet of water in an aquifer. Three sides of the valley are rimmed by mountains that include some of the highest peaks in Colorado. A contrast in vegetation occurs between the disturbed areas and the more natural undisturbed areas on the valley floor. Native grasses such as Indian ricegrass, ring muhly, and blue grama still exist in areas, where in the more disturbed areas, sagebrush, greasewood, and prickly pear cactus have taken over. There are wet meadows that appear out of nowhere and wetlands between sand dunes that seem almost miragelike.

Bison once grazed the wet meadows, and pronghorn are native to the valley. Bison have reappeared on the Conservancy's Medano-Zapata ranch and roam freely on thousands of acres once beat down by cattle ranching. The flat floor of the valley and the surrounding uplands and foothills are home to an astounding mix of Western wildlife. Elk herds, pronghorn, black bear, coyote, mule deer, and mountain lions call the valley home. Wildlife refuges and the Medano-Zapata ranch are birding meccas.

But the key to conservation in the San Luis Valley is WATER. "*The human and natural history of the San Luis Valley can be written in the pursuit, acquisition, and control of water*" (Huber and Larkin 1996).

Even though it is classified as high desert, there are vast amounts of runoff that flow into the valley, mostly from snowmelt in the surrounding mountains. Rain and snowpack dictate how much the aquifer recharges each season. It's a delicate balance and can quickly become a serious ecological and agricultural issue when the precipitation in the mountains is lacking. Surface irrigation and deep well, pumped irrigation support both the ranching communities and the barley and potato farmers in the area. This delicate balance of sharing the water between the human community and the natural community is the conservation issue in the San Luis Valley—that is, until the threat by large corporations to buy ranches (along with their very valuable water rights and pump the water elsewhere to support development) reared its ugly head in the last half of the twentieth century. This continues to be the battle—and is a complex issue, day in and day out, for various conservation organizations and sportsman's groups. Leading the way was and still is the Nature Conservancy. When the sale of the Medano-Zapata ranch seemed inevitable, TNC stepped in and, with the help of a conservation-minded landowner and very generous members, purchased this 103,000-acre cattle and bison ranch adjacent to the Great Sand Dunes; shortly after that, my second Colorado adventure began.

Originally, I was fortunate enough to be hired to establish an environmental education facility and inn at the headquarters of the renovated Medano-Zapata ranch. During the next few years, my duties extended into the project director of the conservancy's San Luis Valley community-based conservation program. Heather also ended up working for the Nature Conservancy in administration.

This became a unique collaboration of conservation groups, ranchers, and farmers, as well as the National Park system, Bureau of Land Management, US Forest Service, and local governments, to protect the water, namely the aquifer, from overpumping and threatening the livelihood of the communities in the valley as well as the rare ecosystems present in this one-of-a-kind special place.

For someone coming from Minnesota, the land of ten thousand lakes, this strange world of water scarcity and water rights was new to me, and it soon became obvious that access to water and water rights does rule the West.

The years my wife and I spent in the San Luis Valley continued to heal my spirit and soul while working to protect the very things that I knew were my secret to healing back to a healthy life. This was not the lush forests of northern Minnesota, but a new kind of natural beauty, a harsh environment struggling to survive in a modern, not so natural, crazy, pro-development world. I could ride out into the heart of the ranch and be alone in this strange new world and get lost in its vastness and solitude.

Sitting on a sand dune, looking down at Sand Creek surging with melting snowpack on the ranch, and watching large herds of elk moving like waves across the landscape couldn't help but calm oneself as you gaze in astonishment at the beauty of the area. Bachelor groups of heavy antlered mule deer walked through the ranch headquarters and around the corrals nearly every day. Mountain lion kills near the house were not uncommon. My camera became a constant companion. I would leave the ranch and hike up into the foothills of the Sangre De Cristo mountains and hunt elk and deer and catch myself just sitting, gazing back down across the sprawling ranches and the sand dunes in a mesmerizing but real daydream. What if the water disappears and the creeks and wet meadows and wetlands that have been here for eons dry up permanently? Would it really matter to anyone other than the ranchers and farmers and biologists in the valley? Most people in the country wouldn't even know. Who even cares about the Great Sand Dunes Tiger Beetle anyway? We could say the same for Mesa Verde, Yellowstone, Acadia, the Everglades, and on and on. But something would disappear with it—something so abstract at times, and hard to describe, that it frustrates me and drives me crazy. It wouldn't be just the landscape and the animals that would be gone, but the chance to sit there or hundreds of places like that and think and gaze and refresh and listen to the *nothing* that our overstimulated brains rarely get a chance to do. These are the places where the recharge, the dreams, the primal feelings seep out of the depths of our soul and surface to make us one again and at peace with ourselves. Where would someone go to forget the ugly, to reconnect with the natural and the beautiful again? What bleak future would it be for my grandchildren, and their children, if all that was left were photos and DVDs and stories of a special peaceful heaven on earth that mankind took for granted, abused, consumed, overdeveloped, and desecrated for sake of our own greed and comfort?

Mountain-fed streams and green ranch valleys and snow-capped peaks—versus blacktop jungles, mass housing, gas and oil wells, and smog filled cities where the only hope of a personal recharge is in a USB port.

That was why I was there. That was why the Nature Conservancy and the Forest Service, and the National Park Service, and on and on were there.

Yes, it was about water, but it was about so much more than just water.

MOUNTAIN LIONS

I've only seen two mountain lions in the wild. Both were in Colorado. Both when I was working with the Nature Conservancy in southern Colorado on the Medano-Zapatta ranch. The first one was during a ride on a narrow-gauge railroad into the foothills of the San Juan mountains. It was an old coal-fired steamer that you could take on a scenic half-day trip from the west side of the valley up into the mountains near Chama, New Mexico.

It was a nice day, so some of us were standing in one of the open cars just enjoying the scenery. I was, of course, scanning the mountainsides and canyons for wildlife with my binoculars. A slight movement alerted me to something across a stream and up on a rocky outcropping. Sure enough, it was a big cat. A classic specimen that was probably napping when this noisy, smokey, soot-belching iron beast came rumbling up the canyon. The large cat had slowly gotten up to stretch, just like a house cat would do on the windowsill after sleeping away half the day in the warm sunlight. His butt was in the air and his front legs stretched way out in front of him. All that was missing was the big yawn. I was only able to watch him a couple minutes as the train doesn't stop. He was in his element, rocky, wild, unforgiving terrain with water nearby, plenty aware, I'm sure, of all the mule deer we were seeing along the way. I then realized I was selfishly hogging the binoculars and handed them to Heather, but by the time she looked, we had passed the window of opportunity and the ledge was no longer in sight. I can still picture it in my head today, like it was yesterday, a memorable first for me.

The second time was on the ranch in the San Luis Valley when Heather and I were with the Nature Conservancy. It was dark and I was driving my truck down from the ranch house where we lived to the corrals on my way to do a night check on the cows during calving time. I took my turn with the ranch hands, as it was a good excuse to be up in the cloudless Colorado night, and besides, it gave them a much-needed break. Just as I glanced up from my coffee, I noticed a pair of yellow eyes reflecting in the headlights of the truck. I hit the brakes hard, even though I wasn't going fast. As soon as my brakes locked up and slid in the sand, the cat ran across the drive and leaped over the fence into the cottonwoods by the corral. I knew there were cats around all the time, but you rarely saw them. We would find mule deer kills relatively often around the ranch buildings and corrals in the cottonwoods, but that was always at night, and the cats would be gone by morning. If only I had had trail cameras back then. We had to be careful letting our golden retriever out after dark because the cats are a real threat to pets. I was used to that discipline because, back home near Ely, in extreme northern Minnesota, we had the same issues with wolves. We knew we were simply a piece of the puzzle here, just like back home, and we loved it.

There is no mistaking a mountain lion if you can see the back half of the body and the long tail. The tails are roughly one-third of the length of the cats, and nothing else has that identifying feature in this part of the country.

I've always been fascinated with cougars, mountain lions, and all top predators.

Now and then in Minnesota, there are reported instances of mountain lion sightings. Most of these cats are coming from the

Black Hills in South Dakota, and typically young dispersing males on the wander. These sightings are more common nowadays with the popular use of trail cameras by all sorts of hunters, hikers, naturalists, and biologists. But most photos are not credited unless the tail is in part of the photo.

In the San Luis Valley, there was a large mountain just to the east of the ranch called Mount Blanca, at 14,345 feet above sea level, the fourth highest peak in Colorado. You would have to travel south all the way to central Mexico to find a higher peak. Blanca is also one of the Navajo's four sacred peaks. It was right out our front window. The valley and the ranch sat at roughly seventy-five hundred feet, the foothills stretching down off Mount Blanca toward the Great Sand Dunes, and were within walking distance, a good hike of the ranch. There was a tree line and a large open meadow way up on the slope that I would watch with my spotting scope from the house and occasionally see elk and mule deer in the meadow. From the first few days we lived on the ranch, one of my goals was to hike up to that meadow and look back down on the valley floor. I think I only tried to make it up there four times while we were on the ranch. It was a long, tough climb, steep and rough with lots of unseen canyons and rock walls and ledges that, of course, you don't notice when looking through a spotting scope a few miles away. I made it to the high meadow twice, once with my golden retriever, Max, the last time alone. At the far edge of that high meadow, I came across a dilapidated cabin. Inside was a spiral notebook tucked into a ziplock baggie. Anyone who found the cabin typically signed the notebook with their name and date. I made two entries about a year and a half apart. There were only a few entries each year, and the older pages were hard to read from the condensation in the plastic baggie over the years. I thought that was one of the coolest things I ever came across while hiking or hunting in the mountains anywhere.

I didn't know at the time, but it would be my last hike to the high meadow; I headed out early one morning alone with a light pack—water and snacks, the camera, and my binoculars. It was a gorgeous day, sunny like most days in the San Luis Valley, just a slight breeze and a fall high temperature around seventy-five degrees. The first part of the hike was up through Pinion-Juniper woodlands and brushy canyons of ephemeral mountain snow fed creeks. The higher you get, the thinner the trees, as you enter an area of rocky draws and canyons. Deer and elk signs were everywhere, and the air was filled with the sounds of pinion jays, scrub jays, hawks, and stellar jays. The only other sound was your own deep breathing as you kept climbing. When you breathe in mountain air at high altitude, it's different from even just down in the floor of the valley. It's clean, clear, piney with a crisp hint of gin like juniper. I remember taking a slightly different route each time as there were no hiking trails to follow. I would generally jump on a game trail that was heading in the right direction and stay on it until it would divert off the wrong way. It was basically boon docking, or bushwhacking.

At one point, I had to backtrack to find a different approach that was passable. I was walking up a steep incline, trying not to slip in the loose, sandy, rocky ground. The slot walls were higher than my head by a few feet, and I was starting to think about the possibility of running into a cat. Soon, the farther I went, it seemed like I could smell something getting stronger. With each step, it became almost overpowering, like your house cat's litter box that hadn't been cleaned out for a week. The walls opened a bit, and I came up on a level shelf in front of a rocky cave. I realized what I was smelling was most likely a heavily used mountain lion area. Another few steps, I saw a partially buried hindquarter of a mule deer in the rocks, and sand with a couple dried out juniper branches over the top. I immediately recognized it as a cat kill. Suddenly the thought crossed my mind that the cat might not be far away, and might be watching me, or worst yet, maybe I had stumbled onto a cat with young kittens in the rocks. I was torn between immediately backtracking out of there or sitting down and waiting to maybe see a cat up close. I waited for a few minutes and then looked ahead and saw that I was close to coming out in the high meadow. So, I got up and continued to walk up into the meadow to the old cabin once more. As I signed the notebook again, I sat there wondering how many times that cat may have walked by and stuck its head through the old door frame of the cabin and looked around. Or maybe even lay up on the mossy old roof of the cabin and watch mule deer or elk graze a few yards below out in the high meadow. I wondered if it ever looked past the meadow, down the mountainside, into the valley, to the ranch, where it had probably hunted at some point in its life. What a perfect spot for a lion. I was the intruder; this was its mountain, and I would go back down to my valley. I took one more long look out and across the wide valley toward the San Juan Mountains in the west, the Great Sand Dunes to the north, and Mount Blanca up behind me.

I wouldn't be honest if I didn't say that, on the hike back down, I stopped a few more times and pulled my backpack up higher around the back of my neck, looking over my shoulder a little more than usual. I love cat country.

PUBLIC VS. PRIVATE LANDS

I t seems like every decade or so there is a discussion of whether public lands across the country should be sold or turned over to the states for management and ownership. This idea apparently goes as far back as when the colonies were formed, and new settlers began to spread out and head West across a country vastly unknown in size as well as unknown in character and geography.

In the early days, people took the huge risk of crossing the ocean in questionable ships to a land of unknowns, escaping the royalty and monarchs and their rules. Land ownership was only for the rulers and families, and in most cases, the richest in Europe. The game on the lands were also owned by royalty and off limits to the lowly peasants and serfs, and commoners. Thus, the lure of actually owning and controlling your own land was almost too much to resist, and worth the risk of getting to the New World.

Most of the Founding Fathers of the country certainly bought into this idea, even though some of them weren't exactly born into poverty.

For the first couple centuries, it seems that the New World was endless and there was no end to the available lands for all. At first, the West was considered anything between the Appalachians and the

Mississippi River. After the original thirteen colonies formed under a new Constitution, they gave the government power to regulate the new lands, which included the power to dispose of and acquire new lands.

Even after the early explorers returned with the news of finally reaching the Pacific, the scale of the country relative to the Old World was just too large to imagine. It was the start of the movement of private ownership in its newest and crudest form. The settlement trend continued with federal acquisition under the Louisiana Purchase, the Oregon Treaty with England, and the results of the Mexican War. In 1862, the Homestead Act reassured the dream, and anyone who could occupy and "improve" the land became its legal owner after a few years. Large unknown areas eventually became territories, and eventually territories became states comprised of private and government-owned lands. Through various acquisitions and disposals, nearly 1.29 billion acres of lands were transferred out of federal ownership between 1781 and 2018—mostly to private ownership, including corporations like the railroads and mining companies, and some to states and Native peoples. Homestead lands reached a peak around 1910 and were fully eliminated in 1986 in Alaska, according to *Congressional Research Service, Federal Lands Ownership Review.*

By the end of the nineteenth century, there was growing concern that this "endless" nation was, in fact, finite, as early environmental concerns started to surface. Among the flashpoints were concerns over running out of the vital natural resources, such as timber and iron ore, and the discovery of undeveloped wilderness lands of natural beauty that should be protected from development. And by the late 1800s, pollution in the most eastern cities was a growing health threat.

The so-called freedom march of exploitation and divide and conquer had run rampant at devastating speed, clearing forests, killing wildlife, damming rivers, and fouling the air we breathed.

Somehow, in this mad scramble in the land of the free, during those decades, individuals like Henry David Thoreau, George Perkins

Marsh, Gifford Pinchot, Adolph Murie, Ansel Adams, Theodore
Roosevelt, John Muir, Aldo Leopold, and countless others emerged
from the population and took bold steps in calling for protection
and care of our natural treasures. These artists, writers, politicians,
scholars, and hunter conservationists came forward with new voice
of reason—a voice that maybe sounded too "Old World" to some,
and too threatening to the new personal freedoms that the nation
had fought so hard to earn.

Thus, the divide began between those who valued freedom and
no government oversight, and those who somehow recognized the
unsustainable appetite the country had for exploiting anything in the
way of so-called progress.

The fear of government control over personal rights and
freedom—or as I call it, the original Big Brother complex, which is
still very present today.

Somehow during all of this, millions of acres of natural wonders,
scenic beauty, wilderness, and areas of historical significance were
somehow miraculously protected by a government in constant flux
of values and priorities and, still even today, in absurd discussions
of who the rightful owner of the federal lands should be, or should
public lands even exist. Some big business, some Western states, and
private-land activists believe all control should go back to the states
where the lands are located, and under absolute state control. If the
states elect to protect, they protect; if they elect to disperse of and
sell off the lands, they have that power to do so.

In this day of budget shortfalls and extreme partisan politics,
the outcomes could be devastating, triggering an environmental and
cultural disaster. Private merely means non-government. Private can
be big oil, timber conglomerates, wealthy private investors, or any
combination of that. States would then control regulations, for the most
part, on any development and building codes or extraction policies.

It wasn't until the passing of the Federal Land Policy and
Management Act of 1976 (FLPMA), that Congress declared that the

remaining public domain lands should remain in federal ownership. That's not to say that lawsuits haven't been tried to change all that, but the courts have generally favored retaining federal ownership versus turning control and ownership to the states—in those cases, a blow to the Sagebrush Rebellion folks.

Even today, the threats are real and on the borders of some of our most treasured places. Just look out from Theodore Roosevelt National Park in North Dakota and see, smell, and hear the massive infrastructure of natural gas and oil extraction adjacent to the park. Toxic copper/nickel mining threatens the pristine watershed of the Boundary Waters Canoe Wilderness Area in Minnesota. Rampant development is cutting off ageless migration routes of animals around our most treasured places.

It would be hard to imagine what private ownership of some of the nation's iconic national parks and wilderness areas would look like. It would be hard to imagine a Disney-World-like Yellowstone, or a private, closed Yosemite, or nonstop helicopter rides into the wilderness areas.

The last remnants of wild remaining in the country need to be there for our physical and mental and social health. Without those areas, there would be no escape, no refuge, no rebuilding of soul and spirit. What a bleak outlook that would be—if we knew the days were numbered where anyone could go find themselves again or explore for the first time with children and grandchildren and plant the ecological subconscious of the next generations.

When the big expanses of wilderness go, there is no hope for the small patches of wild and semi-wild retreats; because, if in our selfish thinking, we can justify desecrating the iconic landscapes that we all know, hope is lost. There would be no elk emerging from the dark timber toward the river. There would be no more arguing as there would be nothing left worth arguing about. I can't imagine living in a world like that; hopefully most people agree. *Keep public lands public!*

THE LONE BULL

Summer 2002

During our time in the San Luis Valley in Colorado, I would often take turns doing duties at the Medano-Zapata with ranch hands. It was a nice break from the inevitable administrative chores to get me out of the office.

I would help with the cattle roundup and branding, the bison roundup, grounds keeping, night patrol during calving season, or any of the other necessary chores on a 103,000-acre cattle and bison ranch.

One of the jobs was to check the aquifer-water monitoring wells across the ranch. They were mapped out, but it was still interesting sometimes finding them in a rolling rabbit brush and greasewood range across tens of thousands of acres.

One morning I decided to check one of the wells out on the far side of the Zapata. I always took the camera along when I moved around the ranch as it was a wildlife mecca. This particular morning, I rode the four-wheeler out past the wet meadows and across a couple pastures and into the rabbit brush. I had been to this well once before, so I had a vague memory of where it was. I rode up to the well and shut off the machine. When I was done, I decided to walk around a little with the camera, just looking at the gorgeous views of the Sangre De Cristo Mountains and Sand Dunes with the ranch buildings in the foreground. I was maybe a hundred yards from the four-wheeler when I crested a small rise and found myself eye to eye with a large bull bison. My first reaction was to pull up the camera and take a shot of the magnificent animal, but I quickly decided that that wasn't a good move, as the shutter noise might irritate the already alert bull. After being around bison for a time, you pick up their body language, and there was no doubt that he was irritated. He raised his tail up and snorted. I knew there was no chance of getting back to the four-wheeler, as an adult bison can outrun a quarter horse. So, I decided to totally submit to the chief; I dropped to my knees and looked the other way to avoid eye contact. We were at a stand-off for what seemed like a very long time, and then I heard him slowly take a couple steps toward me.

Bison have a deep, guttural grunt that sounds like a cross between an African lion growl and a beast from another world. At this point, I knew we were only a few feet apart, and I could smell his breath and body odor in the breeze. The rut was done, and so my only hope was that he was just a little miffed at being disturbed and would take my cowardly stance as a peace offering and just walk off.

Now, if any of you farm and ranch folks have been around cattle, you undoubtedly have been snotted or coughed on. It's not a pretty sight or smell or feeling as it smacks you like a hard slap across the face, only with slimy gooey nasty puss-like stuff. Well, good old chief burped up a good one and coughed. Unfortunately, I was downwind at close range and took a direct hit on the side of the face and neck. He then stretched out his neck and gave me the sniff test. I wasn't sure exactly what I was feeling, as neither fight nor flight was an option. Apparently, I passed the sniff test, and he slowly ambled off toward the four-wheeler. If it was today, I could have taken a selfie with the fresh bison goober hanging from my face, but I instead pulled off the dust handkerchief around my neck and wiped off the gift.

As the old bull walked off toward my four-wheeler, he was

literally standing between me and my getaway car. All I could do was sit there and watch as he slowly worked over the machine, using it as a rubbing post, breaking the taillight as he did so. Then, in a rage, he hooked it and lifted it up on two wheels and tipped it on its side. Bison, two—me, zero! Satisfied that he had totally humiliated me, he slowly sauntered off.

It wasn't uncommon, every so often, that a few of the older bulls would wander off on their own away from the herd or bachelor groups. This apparently was the case, as this old boy was a couple miles south of where he should have been on the ranch. Now and then we would get a call from the Great Sand Dunes or the town of Crestone about a large bull wandering around like it owned the place. It's a little difficult to tell the local sheriff that it's not ours when there wasn't another bison herd on this side of the mountain range.

I still have the quick photo I took, and every time I see it again, it seems like yesterday, and it brings a smile to my face.

WHAT IS WILDERNESS

For a longtime, I've been thinking about the exact meaning of *wilderness*. What does it mean? What is wild? What do most people think of when they think of wilderness? Or, do most people even think about wilderness? A few years ago, I wrote a short essay on wildlands for the International Wolf Center. I was on the board of directors at the time, and we were grappling with the idea of what wildlands and wilderness meant. In the essay, I was focusing on wolves because of the organization I was involved with, but you could substitute almost any other apex predator and the point would be nearly the same. Here are a couple paragraphs from the essay:

> We cannot talk about the survival of any wild species, especially the wolf, without considering habitat, and to me, natural habitat means wildlands. This doesn't necessarily mean wilderness habitat—entirely uncultivated and uninhabited— but perhaps rather a combination of federal, state, and private lands that represent quality environmental conditions, as they would exist naturally in a specific geographic area.
>
> When you include private lands in a habitat equation,

things can get complicated. But it must be included, because most large species cannot survive and expand on the fragmented remnants of government-owned lands that dot this country. Large predators require a combination of habitat that supports prey species like deer, elk, and moose—species that create good hunting for apex predators, such as wolves (substitute grizzly, mountain lion, among others). Private property forms the land links that connect the protected wild areas.

It makes sense, then, when discussing large carnivores, to look at the larger, "landscape-sized" picture, including the compatible areas of habitat that lie adjacent to or nearby the protected or wilderness areas.

This discussion ultimately leads to the topic of development by humans. Can we preserve enough quality habitat outside of protected areas to meet the long-term needs of a wide-ranging animal without increasing wolf-human conflict?

In a positive trend, there are areas in the western US where wildlife population dynamics are an integral part of local land use planning. Wildlands are recognized as a vital part of the social and economic desirability of a given area.

Wildlands and their preservation should not be of concern only to biologists or wildlife enthusiasts. Wildlands bolster the primitive human spirit, clear the mind, and strengthen the soul. Minnesota author Sigurd Olson said, "Joy comes from simple and natural things: mists over meadows, sunlight on leaves, the path of the moon over waters . . ."

To that, I would add, and the howl of the wild wolf.

My point was that, if we are to have space for wild things, then it is going to take collaboration between multiple disciplines of outdoor enthusiasts, fishermen, hunters, horseback riders, ATV users, hikers, photographers, skiers, federal and state governments, nonprofits, and many more.

In my head, I can see a difference between wildlands and wilderness.

In my mind, wilderness areas are already protected at the highest level, the highest rank of public land. Wildlands are natural areas, whether public or private, and have attributes similar to my above description. Yet, they may or may not be protected. These are the links, the connection between the protected government lands and other healthy, high-quality habitats—links that are more important every year. As Leopold put it way back in 1940s, "Many animal species, for reasons unknown, do not seem to thrive as islands of detached populations." A clear early argument for public lands.

For the moment, let us not get hung up on labels and scientific definitions. More important is what it means on a personal level. If people cannot connect to the outdoors and nature, then keeping it wild is all but impossible.

This is not a new discussion by any means. Here are some great thoughts on wilderness:

"Here is your country. Cherish these natural wonders, cherish the natural resources, cherish the history and romance as a sacred heritage, for your children and your children's children. Do not let selfish men or greedy interests skin your country of its beauty, its richness, or its romance."

—Theodore Roosevelt

"Wilderness is the one kind of playground mankind cannot build to order.

"Like winds and sunsets, wild things were taken for granted until progress began to do away with them. Now we face the question whether a still higher 'standard of living' is worth its cost in things natural, wild, and free."

—Aldo Leopold

Gene Hill, in his book *Hill Country*, has a less grandiose idea of what wilderness is, but equally as relevant and meaningful:

> *"We must have our little wildernesses, no matter what size they are, no matter where they would in reality sit on a map.*
>
> *"Wilderness, when you're hungry for it can start almost anywhere. It's that invisible line we cross from the everyday to the out-of-ordinary.*
>
> *"Wilderness is that odd feeling that comes over us, every once in a while, in some quiet spot: a sensation of sureness, of strength, of an almost forgotten feeling that we could really cope, we could have made it anytime—anyplace."*

I have felt that sensation of sureness, that sensation of strength—a strength that we can really cope. I believe that before we can really come together as a whole and agree on our scientific connections and corridors, as mentioned above, we must first come together in our minds with what wilderness is, and what it really means to us as individuals. That's the fire that has to light in us and then cause us to speak about it, yearn even more for it, and work to save it. It must be a thing of our soul, a gut-wrenching awareness of our place in the world and our need for wild places to exist—so that it becomes part of our being. If it is, in fact, a part of you, then it is only natural to defend it.

In the film, *The Hunter*, Ryan Youngblood so aptly says, "In the dark of man, a fire burns. . . . Take in the beauty of nature, and let it in turn take you in."

We are all part of this earth, this planet; all living things together are part of the whole. We are the hide of the earth. We can be that which holds the planet together and protects it, or the cancer that slowly and indiscriminately destroys it forever. We lose something extremely vital to our human psyche every time we rope and brand a piece of the wild.

THE HUNTING AND CONSERVATION DEBATE

Volumes have been written on this controversial subject, and volumes more could and will be written in the years to come. It's a delicate subject, extremely emotional for both sides, and difficult for even good friends and family to discuss sometimes. It automatically becomes more of a hunting versus anti-hunting conversation—with both sides claiming theirs to be true conservation.

I hunt. I enjoy hunting. Some of my children hunt. Some of my friends hunt; some do not. I see a real value in different ways of hunting. I am also a natural resource conservationist. I understand the role hunting has played in this country, both good and bad. I am not anti anti-hunter, any more than I am anti-Lutheran, anti-Methodist, anti-Republican, or anti-Democrat. I don't despise or avoid those people; I have a lot of friends and family who, when push comes to shove, are not real big fans of hunting *anything*. As I said before, I come from a non-hunting family.

Like a lot of controversial topics, to me, it is about the willingness on both sides to not only hear, but actually *listen* to the thoughts and feelings of the other side. In some cases, it may seem impossible to even attempt to understand the logic and feelings behind the emotional arguments. The key word here is *feelings*. As emotional as I get about what hunting means to me and how it has helped me battle through my struggle, there is just as much emotion on the other side that we most often overlook or dismiss. It's too easy, and much safer, to just write off one side or the other as crazy, redneck, killing fools, or greenie tree-hugging wimpy vegans. Before it even starts, the battle lines are drawn, and there is no turning back, no surrender, no listening, no compromise, so, no win. As hunters and nonhunters, we should all be conservationists, and if we want true widespread "buy-in" from the public on saving this planet, then we need to get brutally honest with ourselves and each other. Let's be honest with everyone.

For example, here's a constant hot topic. I went to Africa in the fall of 2019 and had a great discussion about this out in the Boma one evening. If lions *aren't* disappearing from everywhere in Africa, let's admit that. Let's admit that there are places and examples where lions or elephants or hippos are doing very well, in fact, in a few cases, too well. Let's also admit there are places where wildlife should be present but are not—because of overhunting, poaching, development, and greedy governments. There remain places where some populations of these animals have outgrown their local habitat. These species can be—and have been in the past—relocated to areas where there is a critical shortage of a species and a desperate need for new animals to reestablish breeding populations and goals for protection. Captive transplanting works, but it's expensive, so most governments can't afford it. Most of the research and action is being taken by NGOs and nonprofits who raise money for these projects from *both* hunters and nonhunters. We have to stop with the commercials and biased press that make one believe there are only fifteen or twenty lions or elephants left in all of the world. Let's celebrate where populations have been restored. This will not hurt the cause; it can actually help. If controlled, big game hunting is helping finance the relocation and protection of some species. Let's admit that and go from there. It seems strange to comprehend, but hunting will continue to support healthy animal populations worldwide, including parts of Africa and the US, just like it has in the past.

We hunters need to think seriously about how and why we hunt, and stop the showy, chest-pounding insanity that we see on cable television shows and YouTube. It wasn't good twenty years ago, and it certainly isn't good today. It is embarrassing to me as a hunter. There are many places where we shouldn't hunt and cannot hunt to sustain wildlife populations. There is hope in hunting films that are extremely well done, and creative, and sensitive, and show the emotions and understanding that goes into a real hunt, as well as the connection between the hunter and the animal and the environment that this takes place in. That's the true meaning of hunting.

There is no argument that the goal for both sides is the same—to conserve and protect our natural resources for all to enjoy. That's the common ground. That's the potential collaboration between all who enjoy wild things. The disconnect from nature in today's society makes it difficult to impress on people the importance of land protection and keeping our planet on a sustainable track.

That first bow I purchased in high school took me into the world of nature farther than I thought was ever possible, and it has helped keep me there. It was just a very natural progression for me. But there are some days that I'm more comfortable with a camera.

We—as a society, and especially as conservationists—need to help each other find their connection, their tool, their avenue to the natural world. That avenue can be a bow, or a camera, a fishing pole, a bike, a teacher, a volunteer, or a book, or a field trip, or a video, or a walk in an intercity green space. Rarely will it be sitting in a fencerow, waiting for the buck in a woodlot. I was fortunate.

There isn't time left for arguing and finger-pointing.

Whether you get around on horseback, on a mountain bike, an ATV, a Jeep, a snowmobile, a pair of skis, a canoe or kayak, snowshoes, a wheelchair, or even your own two feet, get out there and spread the word. Whether you go out with a fly rod, a fishing pole, a camera, a bow, a rifle, a pair of binoculars, your dog, a backpack, skis, trail shoes, or just the shirt on your back, spread the word.

There is enough space out there for everyone—if we work together and help protect those spaces.

ON MY BACK

Years ago, I took a photo while lying on my back and looking up through the broken canopy of the trees to a beautiful blue sky. I know right where it is still today—the tree, I mean. The place. The right position. I could retake the same image today.

After I shot the photo, I set the camera on my chest and just lay there. The light and dark greens of the aspen leaves framed the endless depth in that deep blue sky. Then the more I looked, the more I saw. Light was reflecting through the veil thin leaves of the trees. Every leaf has a middle vein, called a midrib, running down the center of the leaf. It helps support the leaf with smaller veins branching out from it. It runs up the length of a leaf toward the tip. As I lay there, seeing the intricate structure of that simple aspen leaf, I couldn't help but wonder about how complex the simple leaf really was. It had infrastructure supporting it, small vessels feeding and watering it, all leading toward its tip, its apex, always pointing toward the light, the sun, the very thing that showcased the leaf in its own translucency. One simple but complex leaf—on a small twig, on a branch, on a single tree, part of the Pando, the large, almost endless group of trees bound together by its common root system, all contributing to one of the most massive organisms on earth, all beginning and ending with that one small green leaf—and now I was somehow connected too, just from lying down on my back.

THE ARCTIC NATIONAL WILDLIFE REFUGE

June 2005

I n extreme northeast Alaska, there is a special place, the Arctic National Wildlife Refuge, the ANWR. Well north of the Arctic Circle, cradling the Brooks Range, there are no roads or signs or airports or traffic jams.

The *Gwich'in* people call it "The Sacred Place where life begins." It is home to the largest land migration route of any mammal on earth, the Porcupine Mountain Caribou herd. The Alaska Game and Fish Department puts the herd population at around two-hundred-thousand animals. Over 180 bird species also call it home for part of their life cycle. It is America's last true large wilderness area, and some say it is the least disturbed and intact ecosystem on earth.

From Presidents Eisenhower to Carter, this amazing ecosystem has grown to over nineteen million acres. It is home to not only the largest caribou herd, but to musk ox, wolves, grizzlies, wolverines, polar bears, and countless other species in a rare blend of mountains, valleys, boreal forest, tundra, and coastal plain. But it was the massive caribou herds that called attention to my wife and I, along with the others rafting the Hula Hula River from the foothills of the north slope of the Brooks Range to the Beaufort Sea and the Arctic Ocean.

Flying over Alaska is incredible. We departed from Fairbanks in a light twin turboprop aircraft, landing in a small village just outside the refuge only to take turns boarding a Piper Cub, two people at a time, then flying up and over the Brooks Range. The journey was off the charts—not the flight charts, the emotional charts! Flying only a few hundred feet above the rocky crevices and bare ridges of the Brooks Range, you could see the ruggedness and wilds of the area and the still snow-packed crevices and slides of the higher elevations in late June. I scanned for sheep, but never saw any while in the air. The Super Cub strained as we finally crested the top of the Brooks Range and began to slowly fly down into the canyons and headwaters of the Hula Hula River. Suddenly, the emerald waters of the snowmelt-fed river began to take shape, and I wondered where on earth this little aircraft is going to set down. Shortly afterward, we landed on a narrow gravel strip of riverbed and came to an abrupt halt. There was not a lot of leeway on a small riverbed in the wilds of the arctic north. We jumped out, pulled our two bags out, and the Cub bounced down the cobblestone and lifted off in a surprisingly short distance. The group reassembled after each flight touched down on the river. When the last of our group of ten, including the river guides, finally watched the Super Cub disappear over the mountain for the last time, I suddenly realized that we were as far from civilization as we might ever be.

June is early spring in the Arctic, and we would be taking advantage of the snowmelt from the Brooks Range to feed the river at enough volume to float the two rubber rafts the entire length of the river, over eighty miles, out to the Beaufort Sea. We set up camp along the riverbank and prepared for our first night north of the Arctic Circle in the largest wildlife refuge in the country.

It was that first evening that we discovered a flaw in our packing list. There is no need for headlamps and batteries in mid-June in the Arctic. Rookie mistake. We laughed as we buried them in the bottom of our dry bags. The sun did little more than touch the horizon the entire trip.

Waking up and looking at your watch to find it is two in the morning and the light is still filtering through the tent is crazy, but we had no trouble sleeping after the long trip in.

We quickly set into a routine of breakfast, loading the rafts, and floating down river. The first few days of the trip, the river was narrow, and the flow was strong as the snowmelt rushed toward the sea. We would pull over for lunch breaks or to view anything too interesting to float by, then continue downriver until evening, then stop and set up a makeshift camp. Each camp consisted of small tents and the two rafts tied upright, serving as kitchen and guide shelter. Multiple times, we stopped and hiked into the foothills—only to be amazed at the abundant forbs, wildflowers, and lichens everywhere. It was a sea of miniatures as far as you could observe. At first glance, what appeared to be a drab, one-dimensional landscape turned into a kaleidoscope of subtle colors and shapes and intricate blends. As we climbed out of the riverbed and up the slope, the blues and yellows of lupine and poppies present a Kodachrome of colors against the greens of the grasses and mosses. Spring means wildflowers in the Arctic—with miles of forget-me-nots, cotton grass, bear flowers, pinkish-red phlox, and a soft landscape filled with the light greens of young willows along the riparian areas.

Rocky outcroppings and large boulders were blanketed with multi-colored lichens like I had never seen before. Looking back south to the stark and gray peaks of the Brooks Range and steep canyons from where we just emerged was such a contrast to these foothills and lesser canyons. Looking ahead downriver, if you climbed high enough, we could already see the vast, flat coastal plains that we would eventually drift into. One morning, while glassing the canyons, I spotted Dall sheep in the distance, and before we hit the river again, two muskox bulls were sparring across the riverbed on a grassy plateau. This had become an experience like no other, and I knew it would just get better as we floated downriver at the mercy of the cold, silty, aquamarine snowmelt from the northernmost mountain range on the continent. There were some stretches of class-two and class-three rapids in the canyons, short fast runs in a clumsy-looking but unbelievably controlled hunk of rubber. Paddling through these and hearing nothing but the sound of powerful water—while feeling the power of the river under your feet—was an adrenaline rush that I'll never forget.

As we continued downriver the next few days, the current slowed as the riverbed widened and began to braid in unpredictable patterns. Every trip down this river was a completely different route as currents and snowmelt are constantly moving the silt and gravel riverbed into abstract channels and helix shapes. As the snow and the ice begin to melt each spring, the newly flowing waters rushing down from the peaks of the Brooks Range cut and carve through the ice-clogged river, leaving large blue-green ice formations the size of buses in the middle of the river, diverting the channel toward a new journey to the sea. Aqua-blue layers of ice taller than any of us were scattered along the riverbed, sometimes with tunnels carved through the middle by the abrasive, silt-filled, rushing water. Some were so clear you could see through them like a filtered lens on my camera. Others were cloudy and filled with gravel and debris from scouring the bottom of the river before finally running aground like a runaway river barge.

This barren desert, as referred to by some clueless politicians and corporate oil execs, is full of life at every turn. The closer we get to breaking out onto the coastal plain, and the larger the view shed, the more the wildlife becomes apparent. Spring and summer are just a few fleeting months, and each species is frantically carrying out its mission in life to propagate its kind. The bird life is incredible. From Arctic terns to willow and rock ptarmigan, I was spotting different bird species continually. The refuge harbored loons, ravens, and multiple waterfowl species, like mergansers, eiders, buffleheads, harlequin, and geese. Rough-legged hawks and gyrfalcon and even golden eagles cruised the skies above the coastal plain. At various locations along the way, we would see Arctic char and grayling finning in the currents, each species signifying the biological health of this unique intact ecosystem.

My only disappointment was when the breakdown rod I had packed along snapped in two on only the second or third cast—the first evening I attempted to fish. No one else brought fishing gear, so my fishing was done. No fresh char or grayling for any of us.

Each spring, the Porcupine River caribou herd migrates north toward the Yukon and the Arctic Refuge coastal plains. It's a treacherous journey with the end goal of timing the arrival to the plains with the calving season. Seeing that was the primary reason I was so excited with this trip. I wanted to witness this epic migration, the record-holding migration of any land mammal in the world.

But our window was short. With only ten days on the river, would we be able to come across at least a remnant herd crossing the plains while floating this river?

When we woke the first morning after reaching the coastal plains, we could see a large fogbank coming in across the tundra from the ocean. As it slowly dissipated, and as we looked toward the distant horizon in the midst of the broken fog, we could see the blue-and-white mirage of the Beaufort Sea coast still miles away. With our spotting scopes, we could make out distant icebergs along the coast across this now griddle flat landscape we would be paddling through to get to our destination. Before we packed up, as Heather and I were standing by our tent, a cow moose with a young calf walked within twenty-five yards of us and headed down into the willows along the bank. I backtracked and found that they had bedded down only a hundred yards from our tent the night before.

Shortly after we hit the river, the banks got smaller, and the river widened to the point where, at times, it was too shallow to float. We all got out and dragged and lined the rafts a few hundred yards to slightly deeper water and current. Suddenly, someone in the front raft pointed ahead and shouted, "Caribou!"

We spotted a sandbar maybe fifty yards ahead and decided to pull up and beach the rafts. Before we had a chance to get there, a string of caribou started to cross the river right in front of us. We gazed in amazement as hundreds of animals ran across the shallow water and sandbars and up onto the green, lush tundra to join the herd. Bulls, cows, calves, and yearlings, some calves so small they had to be just days old. The cows would break the current upstream, and the calves would run along just downstream of the cow, sometimes neck deep in the cold melt. I watched in wonder as I realized this was something very special—how fortunate we were to be witnessing this phenomenon here in person in the Arctic National Wildlife Refuge. This exact act happens nowhere else on earth. I was so transfixed that I didn't even think about my camera for the first few minutes.

We stopped at the sandbar after the last of the stragglers had crossed the river and decided to set up camp on the tundra some distance from the river crossing. We watched the herds continue to cross the river, moving almost nonstop, grazing as they went. It reminded me of the way bison move and graze. Some of the caribou would rest on the patches of snow still left, most likely to better escape the relentless swarms of flies and mosquitoes. As we watched and glassed the low hills surrounding the area, we could see a few wolves trailing the herds along the edges, waiting for a sign of a limp or a slow animal falling behind, or a young calf away from its mother. It was unadulterated, unhampered nature in its raw, truest form. We eventually fell asleep listening to the continuous hoofbeats of the endless herds moving across this open, unscathed wilderness— experiencing a glimpse of what they have done for eons.

The next day, we were still seeing herds out across the plains as we reluctantly pushed toward the Beaufort Sea. It was on one of those last days that we saw an Alaska Department of Fish and Game helicopter flying up the river over us. That evening, as I sat around the camp with the guides, they said that it wasn't a good sign to see a chopper heading up the river. It wasn't until we reached our destination at the Eskimo village of Kaktovic that we were informed that a native couple floating down the river a day ahead of us was attacked and killed by a grizzly while they slept in their tent. We unknowingly had floated past them the following day without seeing their camp up on the tundra flat. Once again, it hit home that this was a wilderness, and with wilderness comes risks. In this environment, humans are not at the top of the food chain. We are just a cog in a large wheel in a natural world unaltered by our presence. Up here, our existence is no more important than the American dipper we saw along the river, or that caribou calf struggling to cross the river. We are a tiny part of the whole—not the whole.

Later that night, while I was in our tent staring through the thin fabric of the roof in the glow of the Arctic night, I realized that, after I heard and saw the helicopter flying upriver, it was the first time a helicopter didn't remind me of the war. The rotor blades slicing through the air with that unmistakable sound, for some reason, didn't trigger memories of that violent place. It always happens when I hear that sound. My soul was at peace that afternoon, in the middle of one of the most beautiful landscapes on earth.

The threats to this magical land are real—too real. The gas and oil industry are knocking on the door at its boundaries, eagerly waiting for the right time and the right political climate to invade this rare and unique ecosystem. Unlike places like Yellowstone or Yosemite, the Artic National Wildlife Refuge is remote and rarely visited by the voting public. This makes it even more vulnerable to the falsehoods and half-truths that claim we need the resources to keep our nation safe and free. It seems so simple to me now—knowing what this sacred place is like, to understand why it is so important to have these places. But without being there, will the public realize its importance ecologically as well as spiritually, for our wellbeing? Who gives a crap about the caribou anyway?

The danger lies in our satellite-like vision of the earth. From up there, everything looks fine. But the soul needs places that are hard to get to, places that exist because we haven't been able to civilize and humanize them, those rare places untouched by our careless hands. I am a different person because that place exists; we all are—whether we know it or not.

AN ISLAND SOMEWHERE

*"I am a rock, I am an island . . . and a rock feels no pain,
and an island never cries."*

—Simon and Garfunkel

Sometimes I feel like an island.

There are advantages in being an island. No one is around you or too close. There would be no danger of hurting anyone. There would be no one to care for, worry about, or protect. Islands can be small and obscure, or so large that no one even realizes they are an island. Small sandy islands are vulnerable to winds and storms and waves and will eventually erode. Large rocky islands can endure more and resist and survive the storms. The problem is, when you find out that those rocks help you defend yourself, it becomes easier to build and rebuild the rocks higher and thicker because it has worked in the past. The rocks become the safety shield, your mind and body's flak jacket.

Like us, an island's survival depends not only on its geology, but also on how rough the water is crashing over and over onto the shore. Calm glassy water can sooth the soul. It reflects the good things around you and quiets the spirit. It doesn't take a lot of wind to stir the water, but calm days are rare, and normal days will have light and variable winds that can normally be watched, heard, and enjoyed.

Stronger winds make an island uneasy and guarded. Storms and high winds and heavy surf are cause for alarm and reaction.

And so goes the daily grind of a survivor. Somewhere deep inside, there is always that battle to escape, or to reach out and open up to those around you. It's safer, less risky, and much easier to go it alone and be that island. But islands can be lonely and dark and self-absorbing. On any given day, we don't get to decide how big or what kind of an island we are. There are days when any ripple in the glassy calm water is upsetting and alarming. There are other days where you feel you could ride into the eye of a hurricane without bother. The unpredictability is the hard part, the wearing part. There are those days you wake up just angry at the world and anything in it for seemingly no reason, which causes alarm and self-doubt. Other times, certain people or words or events trigger that anger, and you immediately go on the defensive. It is the most helpless feeling we can have.

I was always a happy kid, enjoying being outside, totally content on playing with others or entertaining myself, especially in the natural world. I still think I am basically a happy person, no doubt happier when I'm outside in a blind or a tree stand, fishing, hiking, or in the kayak, or stalking with the camera.

I've always been happier and more comfortable outside, but it's more than that now. Maybe now it's that beauty and quiet and the complexity of nature that reassures me that there is good in the world. Maybe that's why I get so frustrated and angry when I see or hear about people or companies trashing the environment for personal gains and needless so-called development. Or politicians preaching we have too much public land and wilderness going to waste. It all becomes so personal, so fast.

Sometimes, if you're lucky and you build a lighthouse, someone special might discover your island. Only if you are lucky, and you find that special person, or that person finds you, and you allow it, can you bring a visitor onto your island. Then you may realize that the island isn't that small. There is room for you and someone else, and opening up to someone will make your shoreline even stronger. Strong enough so you can actually sit on a rock and watch those heavy waves crash against you and just fall back away.

HOME TURF

I often think about how strange that war was. In some ways, we were the invited "invader" of sorts. In other ways, we invited ourselves. What was so odd, now that I think about it, is that the North Vietnamese Army had no home bases or established occupied territory in South Vietnam. Yet, they absolutely knew where all of ours were, maybe with the exception of a few small temporary Special Forces camps. Because of that, they could repeatedly attack and shell our fire support bases and headquarters, outlying bases at will, but yet never really succeed in occupying any of them.

We, on the other hand, had to constantly rely on intelligence from the field and, in most cases, literally go out and look for contact in the endless search and destroy missions that were an almost daily occurrence.

That fact was a huge strike against us from the start, and I continue to be amazed at the fact that US forces were so successful in defending the occupied areas. Had the tables been turned, the war may not have lasted long. That is the oddity of guerilla warfare. How can an out-gunned inferior enemy, who essentially never won a battle, hold on and "win?" Although I'm not sure "win" is the appropriate term when referencing either side. It's extremely difficult for anyone who served over there to hear someone talk about how we lost that war. I immediately become defensive and angry. After what everyone went through over there, and dominate like we did, it just seems so incomprehensible to imagine losing the war. If it was a loss—and it certainly didn't go into the history books as a win—then in most veterans' minds, it was the politicians, and the pressure from the public who were sick of the war, that caused the withdrawal of troops from the country, and thus the default "loss" of the war. We threw in the towel and forfeited the win.

Vietnamese author Bao Ninh wrote about his experience in serving with the "Glorious 27th Youth Brigade" of the North Vietnamese Army. Of the five hundred or so who went to war with the brigade in 1969, he was one of ten who survived. His book, *The Sorrow of War*, is an extremely graphic account of what he and his fellow soldiers went through fighting US forces in Vietnam. It was in reading this difficult book that I realized how demoralizing and senseless the war was to the other side as well. He speaks of relentless airstrikes, napalm attacks, and the overpowering, highly trained enemy force that so dominated every aspect of that war. His personal account of doubt, misery, and suffering really struck me and made me start to imagine what it would have been like on the "other" side.

I really don't think that most of the villages we went through really cared about the war, about who would win the war, or who was fighting the war. They just really wanted to be left alone and continue to do what their families had done for hundreds of years. In most cases, their only connection were sons and fathers conscripted to fight on one side or the other and how they could avoid getting caught in the middle of a fight. I honestly think that the Viet Cong villages were only friendly to Viet Cong because they were getting some level of security from them, or their sons ended up fighting on that side. I don't believe that there was any more allegiance to one side or the other. The "friendly" villages were typically close to American bases or posts and sought security and, in some cases, jobs from the Americans. Out in the countryside, loyalty would vary depending on the day and who was around. To a point, I don't blame those villagers for playing both sides. Ideally, the small villages just wanted to be left alone, and had no more stake in the American war than they did in the French war. They could be beat down by us or the Army of the Republic of Vietnam or by the Viet Cong or the regular North Vietnamese Army. It must have seemed all the same. I think about a small boy who came up to me one day while we were on road security out somewhere. We were on the outskirts to what was considered at the time a friendly village. The kids were always begging for something. I gave the boy a candy bar. A short time later, he came back carrying a much younger child with a stump where his leg should have been. I didn't have any more candy bars, so I gave them a can of peaches and a can of pound cake. I remember the expression on their face, like I had just given them a million bucks. I thought a lot about those kids that night, wondering who was responsible for the kid's injury and suffering, *us or them*, and it certainly didn't matter to the kids at that point. I never smoked, so sometimes I would give my four-pack of cigarettes to kids so they could sell them back to the guys or other villagers, or in some cases, they smoked them. Other times, I would hang on to the four-packs that came in every box of C rations, as they were extremely valuable merchandise in the field.

Uniforms and flags don't change the long-term effects of war on those who survived it, regardless of which side you were on.

I've never gone back to Vietnam, but maybe someday. For years, I had absolutely no desire to return. I understand how former soldiers from both sides have met and embraced and wept and sat down together years after their battles ended. It must be an overwhelming emotional and healing experience. To me, that says wonders for the human spirit.

THE GOOD
ELEPHANT HUNT

I want to tell you a good elephant story this time. It's from one of my favorite outdoor books, by author Gene Hill. Gene was the kind of writer who ordinary guys could relate to, often times writing about simple things. You would catch yourself smiling when reading his stories. It wasn't until after I had read five of his books that I found out he had served in Okinawa in the military during WWII, and then came back and graduated from Harvard. That shows you the kind of individual he was.

One of Gene's stories was about a friend who was an avid big game hunter and had gone on more than a few African safaris. His friend, over time, became obsessed with hunting an elephant. I mean, really obsessed. He read everything he could get his hands on about elephants and talking with people who had hunted elephants. Shortly after being diagnosed with cancer, his friend finally got his chance to go on safari with an elephant hunting outfitter in Nairobi. The hunt became a painful long walk—nearly two weeks tracking a huge bull elephant. As the hunt went on, he began to identify with the large bull. He was patterning his moves and predicting where he would go next. He and the animal had almost become one, "linked together by destiny that neither could avoid." As they finally started closing in on the elephant, the hunter and his guide moved ahead to a waterhole, guessing that's where the large animal would be heading. Near dark, he saw the elephant standing at the edge of a clearing near the waterhole. He then realized that the elephant had most likely been watching him, the hunter, for quite some time. As they stood looking at each other, he realized the elephant had only one tusk. He could only imagine how the huge bull must have broken the tusk off in an ugly battle. He brought the rifle up and paused, looking across at the old battle-scared monarch. Then he slowly lowered his rifle and just stood there looking at the bull. After a short time, the bull turned, as if to acknowledge him, and slowly walked back into the dark canopy of the forest.

When Gene Hill's friend had finished telling him the story, he said, "Perhaps, when all is said and done, we come to learn that the greatest pleasure in owning a gun is discovering the great privilege of not using it."

Honest and true hunters realize the power that they possess, and acknowledge this to themselves, knowing what the result of pulling the trigger can bring. Sometimes the shot comes quick; sometimes the shot comes after long and hard journeys. And then, sometimes, maybe just sometimes, we lower our arms and watch our elephant walk away.

EPILOGUE

The United States continues to lose natural lands at an alarming rate. According to a recent report from the Center for American Progress (CAP), the US lost a football-sized area of natural land to development every thirty seconds between 2001 and 2017. It continues today. The losses are preventable, it claims, but it will require a serious shift in perspective and serious effort to conserve and protect America's wildlife and natural spaces. Only 12 percent of all US land is currently protected by law, according to Conservation Science Partners (CSP). The US Forest Service states that each day an estimated six thousand acres of open space is converted to other uses.

Different studies all come to the same grim conclusion. We are losing the collective soul of wilderness by the acre, by the day. The worldwide picture is even more tragic and alarming.

How can we ignore such alarming statistics? It's because these numbers mean nothing to those who can't or have never experienced anything remotely close to wild nature. Most of our society is deprived of the experience that some take for granted. The future looks bleak unless we as a society embrace each other and recognize our primal need for comfort and peace from the natural world. Until we realize that, we will hurt. Deep down in every human soul is the need for the spiritual and emotional healing that only nature can provide.

I am here because I am lucky; I am here because I have experienced the need and the emotion of nature's healing power. I have felt the power rebuild my tired soul. This is my new battle.

CPSIA information can be obtained
at www.ICGtesting.com
Printed in the USA
JSHW020851170722
28120JS00004B/19